ENTERING
THE REAL WORLD

WAVERTREE PRESS

ENTERING THE REAL WORLD: VCCA POETS ON MT. SAN ANGELO

Margaret B. Ingraham

Andrea Carter Brown

Editors

WAVERTREE PRESS

Wavertree Press

an imprint of

Virginia Center for the Creative Arts

154 Mt. San Angelo Drive

Amherst, Virginia

ISBN: 978-0-9833142-9-5

VCCA is supported in part by grants from

the National Endowment for the Arts

and the Virginia Commission for the Arts

ART WORKS.
arts.gov

VIRGINIA
COMMISSION
for the *Arts*

Cover photography

Front: *VCCA Studios in Spring*, 2002, Bernard Handzel

Back: *The Real World*, 2011, Karen Bell

Cover design

Lexie Boris

Contents

Poems

Foreword

by Kelly Cherry

"The world is too much with us," wrote William Wordsworth, and many of the poems included in this splendid, intriguing anthology share that sentiment. The poets whose work is herein presented have at various times resided at the Virginia Center for the Creative Arts in Amherst, Virginia. The entrance is almost hidden. A narrow, curving driveway climbs Mt. San Angelo, passing carefully placed, surprising stelae and sculpture, to a simple dormitory, a view of the Blue Ridge Mountains ("Blue mountains loom abroad, the muses' Ararat," writes Jennifer Rose in her "Virginia"), and grounds as beautiful as a Cézanne landscape. In fact, VCCA visual artists have painted aspects of this scene many times over the years. Given thick-trunked trees, a fenced pasture, a barn complex revised into studios, boxwood hedges, and a gazebo, the arriving Fellow encounters "glimpses that would make me less forlorn," as Wordsworth said, glimpses "of Proteus rising from the sea; / Or hear old Triton blow his wreathed horn." Some quality of mythology lingers: not the old, but what Ezra Pound had in mind when he urged writers "to make it new." There is a desire to advance understanding by making works that are fresh and forward-looking while expressing in its full range the human condition. Here, the creative artist working in any medium escapes a jangling, distracted world and finds a space in which to think, feel, edit, and shape. The transition from the real world to such a magical location is sudden and shocking, and emergent themes in the anthology at hand are the rediscovery of peace and quiet; renewed and grateful awareness of nature (from the horses in the pasture to the bark beetle that sits on a manuscript); a collective concentration that makes of the artists a community; and simultaneously an opportunity to explore one's own mind.

Thus, while sharing certain themes, each poem here is different from every other. Such multiplicity in a themed volume is exceptional. In the first poem, "Spring Comes to Virginia," Marcia Aldrich paints a word-portrait of a poet departing still-wintry Michigan and traveling south to the colony. Karren LaLonde Alenier's "Retreat," also set at the colony, is less bucolic than ironic and angry, protesting the slaughter of cattle. Andrea Carter Brown gives us "Blues, for Bill," a heartbreaking elegy for the late and much-missed poet William Matthews. Andrea Hollander Budy, on the other hand, in "Writing Studio," offers a caveat: the poet is not a "god / free to invent the world" so much as simply someone who gleans what he can "but only after the crows / have finished," words to take seriously. And Deborah Cummins tells us:

> Here's a log mapped with lichen
> light hasn't touched yet. We can sit
> at an easy distance, nothing between us.
> (from "Before It's Too Late")

Barbara Crooker's title "The VCCA Fellows Visit the Holiness Baptist Church, Amherst, Virginia" may lead us to expect something a little twee, or superior-sounding, but is a wonderfully big-hearted, full-throated celebration of people coming together, "visitors and strangers enfolded / in the whole, like raisins in sweet batter."

"Knowledge of Cows" by Steve Roberts, a perfectly gorgeous poem, celebrates the ordinary: rocks, a pond, air, a fence, leaves, a shrub, robins, shadows, a snake, and of course, cows. Cows are a rampant subject at VCCA, because its neighbor and associate, Sweet Briar College, has a herd of them.

The reader must not think, however, that this anthology comprises *only* pastoral poems. There is no greeting-card verse here. The poets who wrote these poems are either well-known or becoming well-known for their craft and intrepidity. George Ellenbogen writes about "Buzzards by a Dead Dog," roadkill being, as a colleague of mine once pointed out, unfailing inspiration for poets. Poets like Charles Fishman, Alice Friman, Con Hilberry, and the distinguished Colette Inez are as alert to the darkness as to the light. Lori Horvitz includes these eye-opening lines in "Art Colony Birthday Party":

> Once I locked eyes with a deer
> and all the ships lost in the Bermuda Triangle
> sailed between us.

Margaret B. Ingraham puts her finger on the full dimension of what poets hope to catch with their lines:

> pillar of cloud will dissolve
> into the gray solitude of cattle
> sighing and that mysterious wisdom
> we came here to know

> will slip invisibly inside
> silence's fence.
> (from "Proverbs")

The Fellow may escape distraction, but nobody escapes tragedy, and some of these poems are written from wounds, powerful and perhaps therefore hard to read. "Lately all that matters is what is missing," Sybil Kollar writes in "The Cows (Sweet Briar)." The accomplished Marilyn Kallet mourns her father but casts a cooler eye on her mother in "Ode to the Open Window (Sweet Briar)." LuAnn Keener-Mikenas memorializes the colony's copper beech tree split by lightning and warns herself to "skip the melancholia." Elizabeth Seydel Morgan's "The Place You Left" is a moving elegy. Neil Shepard tells us "This Is How It Is," this life, this journey endward. The young and full-of-feeling Taije Silverman, in her wise poem "On Joy," reckons with faith and loss, but concludes, "*Look*. We're standing in a field." Memye Curtis Tucker offers a portrait of a pianist "playing now / in counterpoint to memory." All these poems and others register the fact of absence, or as the admirable Alison Townsend puts it, "the great and ordinary mystery of being mortal."

VCCA is, as we noted, a community, and some of the poems observe its workings and those of a larger society. Becky Gould Gibson's "Summer Solstice in Pastels" illustrates how one art influences another. Halvard Johnson in "Old Virginia Trees" is characteristically witty and sardonic, calling our attention to the dishonesty of pre-packaged language, the futility of cheerful slogans; he is a poetic George Orwell. Ginny MacKenzie records with vivacity and sorrow a confrontation between two very different persons ("No Leash Law"). Mary Mackey's excerpt from "Lynchburg" makes a vigorous statement about the horror of the Civil War. Kathleen O'Toole's "Winter of Ice and Straw" employs memorable diction in a poem that begins in Virginia and moves to Afghanistan, where a family is "making bread of grass, their final hedge against famine." Melissa Stein writes "Anaphylaxis" against suicide, for life.

Finally, there are poems of forgiveness. Perhaps the peacefulness that so many feel in this place encourages forgiveness, including forgiveness of oneself. Stephen Tapscott's "Mud" comments on prayer as a "specific longing, as if the forgiveness I pray toward / would be a specific forgiveness and I will know when it comes." "Stillborn" by Marjory Wentworth is empathic and unforgettable. Poet and fiction writer Enid Shomer takes a feminist stance in "Among the Cows" to endow us with these remarkable lines:

> I want to believe I could live
> this close to the earth, could move with

a languor so resolute it
    passes for will, my heart riding
low in my body, not this flag
    in my chest snapped by the lightest
breeze. Now my breath escapes with theirs
    like doused flames or a prayer made
visible: May our gender bear
    us gracefully through these cumbrous frames.

Leaving VCCA, taking the narrow road back to the highway, colonists see a sign that says "The Real World," yet most will say that VCCA *is* the real world, the other being a place of confusion and discord—or maybe it's just a bit trivial in comparison.

A few poems in this anthology deal with the return to the "real world." Martin Tucker's "On Leaving an Artists' Colony" is both funny and touching. The final poem, "Night Vision" by Michele Wolf, recalling an image of an unnamed "Us"—"Our bridged, wavering image / On the water, pale and indistinct"—closes the anthology on a lovely, muted note.

There are over sixty poets here and they represent many countries; their names and contributor notes will make it clear that VCCA has made its mark felt worldwide. VCCA is international in scope, local in feeling, and exists, for the artists, in a timeless universe. I would like to name every poet in this collection but, with so many, have been obliged to choose some to indicate the distinction and diversity of the whole. All of them are important poets; all of them are exciting and adept. Their work brings us not only the "real world" but the real stuff.

Mt. San Angelo

September, 2011

Preface

by Suny Monk

Writing the preface for this anthology is both a striking professional opportunity and an exercise in overcoming writer's block. But trying to find words that will do justice to the work of our cherished Fellows— Kelly Cherry, the Poet Laureate of Virginia, Peggy Ingraham whose life and poetry have so often moved me beyond mere words, and the 59 other writers who create wonder, seems to have struck me dumb.

But certainly I can write of the importance of this place. I hear it from the Fellows daily: the power of the silences, the thrum of the mountains, the serenity radiating from the red soil. It is the luxurious length of days at Mt. San Angelo that knits together the complex ideas only glimpsed in the rush of the real world. The poetry in this collection speaks of the balance between the human community and solitude and of how the roaring quiet of a closed studio door invites ideas that are only imagined when the world is too present in our days.

During the forty years of her existence, VCCA has given this treasure of intellectual freedom to over 4500 worthy writers, artists and composers. She has been an artistic touch point, a crucible, the crux of so much unexpected new work. If there were ever a "memoir" written of every bit and piece, imagine the collection it would create.

Her gift doesn't stop there. As staff members, VCCA has changed our lives too. The new work and wonderful people that we discover at the dinner table, on our evening walks and at studio visits have polished the talents we bring to VCCA and opened our minds to be better observers, listeners and interpreters.

I am so thankful to Peggy Ingraham who brought the idea of this anthology to life. A collection of poetry seemed an appropriate anniversary gift from our writers, but a collection of work *evoked by* VCCA was the stroke of brilliance. Peggy gathered talented assistance, most notably that of gifted co-editor Andrea Carter Brown, to bring this volume to print. Published in this 40th anniversary year, it celebrates the first two generations of VCCA writers. I think of it, too, as a culmination of my fifteen-year tenure at its helm. What a gift those years have been! With its publication I trust that this anthology will launch the next decade of inspiration.

The spirit that *is* Mt. San Angelo lives in the creative lives of our Fellows, our staff and all those who have been nurtured by her. Beyond her closest circle, the spirit flows into the world, giving a glimpse of the creative life on this magical hilltop. I know it will open the window to a place in your heart as it has for 4500 Fellows.

Mt. San Angelo
September, 2011

Introduction

by Margaret B. Ingraham

While I was in residence at VCCA in 2009, the first *WetPaint!* event took place in Charlottesville and I had the joy of participating. *WetPaint!* was a large reception and silent auction of work that VCCA visual artists had donated for sale. For me it was an extraordinary opportunity to see firsthand the kind of energy and response from the public that could be generated when they were exposed, at one time, to a large body of diverse work by dozens of visual artists who had been VCCA Fellows. The event not only produced energy and interest but also a substantial amount of financial support for VCCA, the full value of which doubtless was just beginning to be counted that evening. And *WetPaint!* also set me to pondering once again what I had asked myself many times before: How could we poets follow the lead of our visual artist compatriots and contribute to helping raise awareness and financial support for VCCA through our work?

The next day back in my studio I picked up the bookshelf copy of the familiar *Best American Poetry*, an annual anthology in which all poets privately or publicly aspire to be included, and I had my answer and the model for this 40th anniversary anthology. I knew from my several residencies the quality of work being produced by VCCA poets—whom Kelly Cherry characterizes in her brilliant foreword to this book as "well-known or becoming well-known"—and I had been moved by how often the poems they offered up in readings for other Fellows made direct connections to the physical, communal, intellectual and creative space we Fellows shared. So I made an appointment to present my idea to VCCA Executive Director Suny Monk and Sheila Gulley Pleasants, Director of Artists Services and staff liaison to the Fellows Council. They embraced the notion but agreed with me that the project itself should be primarily a volunteer one, organized and carried out by Fellows, not staff, and sponsored by the Fellows Council.

A call for poems was announced and the interest from Fellows and the response as measured by the number of submissions was astounding. For me and Andrea Carter Brown, whom I recruited as co-editor the day she was elected to the Fellows Council in 2010, the task of selecting which of the pieces to include in *Entering the Real World: VCCA Poets on Mt. San Angelo* was at once ecstatic and agonizing. It was the former, of course, because the response was so enthusiastic and the work so outstanding. It was agonizing because, in the end, we could not accept all the poems generously offered. As poets ourselves, who have received our fair number of rejections, we knew the pain that could inflict; and we knew in this case, because we were responding "in the family," the sensitivity of our role was heightened. With that full knowledge, we did our best to carry out our editorial role compassionately and fairly, and we recruited other skilled readers so that each submission was reviewed by four or five individuals. Our thanks extend not just to those poets whose work we include here, but to all who offered poems for consideration.

As one who has been living with the poems in this anthology for nearly a year now, I am pleased to declare unabashedly that I believe it achieves something almost mystical. And it does so not simply because the work collected here is some of the finest poetry, published in many of our best literary journals as well as individual collections, over the past four decades, but because all of the poems included are connected directly to VCCA. To clarify: that does not mean that every or any poem here is a "place" poem as Kelly Cherry articulates so well. But it does mean that every poem is tied back to VCCA, that real and mysterious world that we Fellows enter when we ascend Mt. San Angelo. Viewed separately or taken together, these poems illustrate what only poetry may be able to convey: the inextricable, undeniable, inscrutable, absolutely palpable, and, yes— mystical—connection that VCCA Fellow poets have to the physical place in which they spend their residencies.

When this poetry project was explained to one renowned poet, she retorted reflexively, "I don't go to artist communities to write about the place." When she said that, she surely was speaking for us all. I don't imagine that any of the poets whose poetry appears here ever came to VCCA to write about VCCA. They came to pursue a new concept or method, or to complete or rework a poetry project in a place where they could spend uninterrupted time with the muse. Frequently, as these poems testify, VCCA becomes the muse, and we poets cannot help but react to the muse's promptings by putting into verse those things being revealed to us in and about the particular creative space we are occupying.

Our "VCCA poems" liberate us from the other unreal world we occupy daily. They are like the breeze that blows the door open and makes way for the literally thousands of other poems that are created here.

Kelly Cherry's insightful Foreword has clearly and skillfully prepared the way for dialogue between the reader and the poems included here, and so they should be allowed to speak for themselves. But I do want to make one observation that attests to VCCA's pioneering spirit that is wholly consistent with the land of both native Monacan and foreign settler that surrounds it. While VCCA cannot and should not shed the charming and deeply Southern and Virginian and Blue Ridge heritage that informs much of its character as an institution, the VCCA community is and always has been a welcoming and fostering place for serious and talented artists from the entire world. VCCA has supported diversity from the beginning, decades before our culture embraced such. Diversity is what the reader will find here. Of age, gender, race, ethnicity, creed, nationality and geography. Of form and method and voice and subject. The birthdates of the contributors to this anthology span five decades, from the 1920's through the 1970's and the publication dates of poems included range across decades as well. This anthology is at once a work of literary merit, a celebratory offering, and an historical record of a hallowed place.

While *Entering the Real World: VCCA Poets on Mt. San Angelo* was in the beginning my brainchild, it could never have come into being without the significant support and contributions of others. First, of course, was the VCCA itself, personified by Executive Director Suny Monk, who embraced the project from the outset, provided the necessary seed money to publish the volume, and pledged the staff's assistance at the various stages. With Suny's blessing and the counsel of Sheila Gulley Pleasants, Director of Artists Services and liaison to the Fellows Council on which I serve, I approached the Council to sponsor this endeavor as an official project. They concurred. From the beginning, Council Chair Karen Bell, who furnished one of the cover photographs, provided an encouraging and shepherding hand to us—the initial "us" being Sheila and Craig Pleasants and myself. Sheila's involvement and contribution cannot be overstated. Her clear focus, dedication and characteristically gracious and unflappable disposition more than once kept the project from foundering. Craig brought a visual artist's perspective: he designed the imprint under which this volume and future VCCA works will be published. Lexie Boris provided critical technical and artistic support in bringing the book through the production stage. So, staff support was substantial and more involved than was originally anticipated. As I noted earlier, Andrea Carter Brown was the last to join our editorial team. Last but not least, the cliché goes, and it rings true here. As co-editor she immediately brought head and heart fully into the project, contributing not only significant amounts of precious time away from her own work but also specific editorial experience and expertise that I sorely lacked. Without Andrea's selfless contribution of talent, time and energy this anthology would not be in your hands today.

Most of all, *Entering the Real World: VCCA Poets on Mt. San Angelo* would not exist without the generous outpouring of submissions from VCCA Fellows, who lent their work without expectation of anything in return. These poems are their individual contributions to the institution they respect and love and the place that informed their work.

Together we celebrate the first 40 extraordinary years of the Virginia Center for the Creative Arts, even as we hope to contribute in some small way to ensuring the vibrancy and vitality of its next 40. We invite you to enter our world.

Alexandria, Virginia

September, 2011

ENTERING
THE REAL WORLD:
VCCA POETS
ON MT. SAN ANGELO

MARCIA ALDRICH

Spring Comes to Virginia

I, who was too tired to begin at the beginning, who wrote *I am a fool and helpless*, needed to be unhinged from my life, to drive slowly, drawing out the time to cross Michigan, down the slow side of Ohio, across Pennsylvania, into Maryland, briefly touching West Virginia and then passing into Virginia; I needed to traverse the flatness of Michigan and Ohio and leave behind their mounds of dirty snow and small square yards of mud, the clenched heart and the congested house, forget the dogs perched at the dining room window and children standing on the front stoop, waving good-bye, climb the snowy altitudes of Pennsylvania with clear cold blue skies above; I needed the ups and downs of the Cumberland Pass, deer at the roadside at dusk the same speckled brown of the rockslides behind them; I needed to be alert to their leaping into the road, the heightened sense of new territory rising before me just as the light failed: it wasn't eternity, it simply had to take time. I needed to break down, run out of gas, lose my way, lose my bags. It had to be unclear if or when I'd ever get there (would I know when or if I'd gone far enough); my hand had to get tired, my brain had to crumble, I had to bend out of the shape I had been keeping. I needed to find a new rhythm —ends hanging fire, me in the middle—bluebells in a glen. Coming through the Blue Ridge Mountains, wheels of winter wheat rolled to a standstill in straw-colored fields, rain-stained stones, forsythia scattered in strong yellow hedges, drifts of daffodils in meadows (daffodils are meant to drift)—a world suddenly brought to my attention—moths, butterflies, birds at rest, lying in nests, in ferns, in tall grasses, dark, rich, deep, illuminated from within; mud the color of red clay, three red foxes running down the wooded hill, horses walking single file in the distance, the blasting horn of the train breaking into another world near midnight, buzzards overhead surveying the upper half of a baby doll thrown in a ditch, its ears and face thick with dirt, the peepers living in a bathtub deep in the woods, deep in rainwater, suddenly silent. How quickly the landscape fills in. Trees whose branches were twisted and stark feather out, a pale kiwi green; the white pears, half dead, flower, their whites mixing with the firs, dabs of soft pink, sunburst yellow, a wash of chalky mustards and lavenders round the necks of trees. I needed to eventually arrive somewhere I'd never been, call it Virginia, far enough away from where I began, where I'd want for nothing, miss nothing, a part preserved almost to the last; I needed a simple single bed, white bedspread of the guest bedroom at a grandmother's house—plain, without color or pattern —where I could lie down on two flat pillows with white cases and hear the arrival of the much-anticipated bluebirds—*the bluebirds are here, the bluebirds are here*, bluebirds on the wire fence, bluebirds inches from my ears. *Wait, I'm not done.* Reluctance to let go of their repeated phrase, even their silences. The house at night on the top of the hill, its beacon lights lit like a cruise ship sailing dark waters, portholes aglow; waves of suddenly warm days, still, without breeze, planet-like bumblebees in a frenzy of lust and then the rains sanding away pear and apple, pushing them back, swirls of petals knocked onto the sodden ground, flattened. How quickly someone will say *It's time to jump in the lake* and it will be nothing like winter, not winter's single pennywhistle, but the delicate smell of jasmine and cut grass on the bend before the road to the barns, not winter's stack of unused white paper, but Virginia crying at my door, filling my room with sun.

from *Northwest Review*, 2003

KARREN LaLONDE ALENIER

Retreat

Outside my studio window, they load
steers into a truck, poke
the animals' flanks with canes,
prod the fleshy beasts up the chute.
The cattle butt one another, stamp
their hooves, rattle the metal
siding. I open my door,
approach the fence,
look for 537,
his ear tag
gone from the yard,
his big eyes bulging.

In the Nation's Capital, I visited
a friend in his secured
government office. "Look
at this," he said, "a captured
cartoon manual instructing Nazi
soldiers how to load what
they called *yids*
into cattle trucks,
gun muzzles jammed
in their ribs." Transfixed,
I bend over his desk. No words:
the guards couldn't read.

In the community where I grew up
skinheads broke into the yeshiva,
tore pages from religious texts, slashed
yarmulkes, smeared fecal swastikas
on the walls. Though apprehended,
no penalty: they all go free.

Back at my studio, I hold
my pen, riffle through
my books, retreat
with history. The farm
settles, 537, so much meat
on the rural ledger.

from *Looking for Divine Transportation*, The Bunny
& Crocodile Press, 1999

ANNETTE ALLEN

After the Ice Storm

*It was one of those places where that
magnificent peacock we call nature seems
to strut before our eyes.*

Victor Hugo

Viewing the Rhine, Hugo knew
the true eye of earth is water, a flowing
form that gives us back the self
hovering beneath divided surface
of rivers, lakes. Here at the Center,
the eye opens to an overnight world,
which shines, intimate, the crystal
branches letting down their hair
in strands of water that mirror sky.

Whatever falls today mesmerizes,
a slice of liquid streaming into the cup,
breath's frosted steam, even magnolia
leaves shattering like glass. Everything
that makes us see, sees, as morning baptizes
this last known stand of longleaf pine,
the drops pooling for the red cockaded
woodpecker, almost extinct, still
living in cavities of old-growth trees.

Listen. If the birds are telling of it,
back and forth through the damp

streets of air, over the ice-glazed
thickets, it's not about the sunlight
ricocheting off the pond's eye where
they drink, but that water remains
distinct after drinking, its skin intact,
and somehow they know they will
come and go, but water outlasts them.

from *Country of Light*, Mount Olive College
Press, 1996

REBECCA BAGGETT

God and the Artists' Colony

Talking at dinner, we discover
how many of us have fundamentalist
families—mothers and sisters

stricken with gifts of tongues, ponderous
deacon fathers, brothers who praise
Jesus for every red light missed.

God rides them, we decide, the way
our art rides us: Perhaps God
is their art, driving them toward that

perfect abnegation, that desire to open
themselves and let Him fill them,
use them, just as we, alone here, locked

in our separate cells, struggle
to surrender self and let our blankness
fill with words, light, music, images

flashing against the dark screen

of our eyes, each of us moving, aching,

toward that private *Alleluia*, revelation,

Yes. . . .

from *Claiming the Spirit Within*, Beacon Press,
1996, and *God Puts on the Body of a Deer*, Main
Street Rag, 2010

NED BALBO

The Minor Hours

The world is all potential; empty rails
That reach from sea to sea or start to tremble
With incoming freight; birds fly from trees—
We don't know where they go—cows slosh through mud
And grass tamped down, lowing along the way,
Escaping to an afternoon that's hushed
Itself, almost, to sleep or nonexistence.
What's their destination? We'll go, too,
Like cows or birds, exactly where we must;
Like trains, where we are sent or finally summoned;
Or, like the cicadas in the trees,
Risen from broods, we'll climb, shaking the leaves
Maple or chestnut, sweet gum, sassafras
With shudders that become our voices, pulsing.

performed by the Brooklyn Conservatory Chorale at
the Lafayette Avenue Presbyterian Church and the
Brooklyn Conservatory Concert Hall, June 2009

MARY BONINA

Lines Inspired by a Horse

A horse trotting to the fence
knows in one lick it's fallen
for the trick of one who comes
empty handed, only wanting kisses.
Tongue rolling, unrolling,
searching for the missing sugar-apple-carrot,
deprived even of a stroke of the mane,
just left to scrounge white clover, to pose
in the middle of the field for passersby.

When I return you will not know me
or you will be blind and deaf
or occupied with the breeze ruffling and fraying
what remains of leaves on the Osage orange,
the rain blasting trumpets of morning glory,
shaking trees so you will remember the clunk
of walnuts falling to the ground.

When you see me again you will seem
so deep in contemplation of stone or mud
that you will not even notice me.
You may pretend or really be sleeping in that way
that seems not like rest for having to keep on
holding yourself up, though your head bows
and your body twitches.

I admit I walked away with sadness
when I had nothing to give, seeing
flies glued like freckles across your nostrils.
I walked away not knowing the payment
exacted, not expecting the disappearing act,
how the gentlest tug can remove an outer layer,
sneak up on you when you least expect it,
how any creature will take
the scent of your clothing as a substitute for you.

from *Clear Eye Tea*, Cervena Barva Press, 2010

ANDREA CARTER BROWN

Blues, For Bill

How fitting that he should come back as blues,
the whole panoply from indigo to ultramarine
on two wings, as cows lumbered up the swale

to a hilltop pasture, the sun sunk behind the now
truly named Blue Ridge, the world in deepening
shadow. How perfect that he should come back

as a butterfly, and yet, given his love of words
and where they come from, how apt it should be
in the blues of a Red-spotted Purple, southerly

conspecific to the White Admiral she might find
in the city where they lived. This is her first summer
in this state; this is the first blue butterfly she's

ever seen. She is wearing blue jeans. She stands
just beyond the shade of a stately Chinese elm,
watching day fade. Except for the cattle, it is

utterly quiet. The butterfly alights on her right hip
and stays, its quivering subsiding slowly to calm.
She could touch it, but doesn't. The Incas believed

warriors fallen in battle visit loved ones left behind
as butterflies, she learns later. She knows very little
of this then. She still doesn't know what happened

to his ashes, his cookbooks and jazz, the last message
she left. She knows where his books went, who took
in Velcro. To satisfy him she learned the difference

between twilight and dusk. She tries not to budge,
to breathe as lightly as she can. With nightfall, he lifts
off. She knows how lucky she is. How lucky she was.

from *Ploughshares*, Spring 2002 and *Blues For Bill: A Tribute to William Matthews*, University of Akron Press, 2005

ANDREA HOLLANDER BUDY

Writing Studio

You guide the thin black stream
across white sand,
stopping now and then
at something invisible, feeding
it, believing something might
actually grow there.

Soon crows arrive,
swirl down, a few at a time,
then more and more,
blackening the sand until it becomes
a field of motion, those black marks
proof there is something
alive in the field, seeds
sending their small shoots up.

People appear—some
relatives and the house
you grew up in, the woods
beyond it, the empty lot.
The voice of your father tells you
to mind your own business.
You decide to remove him,
bring in your mother instead.

Do not fool yourself.

Do not think yourself
some all-powerful god
free to invent the world
according to your whims.
You are a watcher
at the edge, a gleaner.
After the harvest is done,
you may take what you can,
but only after the crows
have finished.

from *The Georgia Review,* 2010

FRAN CASTAN

Giant Beech at Sweet Briar, February

Think of a dozen elephant legs,

draw them close,

and you have the base. Look up.

Black burrs, heavy-lidded, look back

as a thousand elephant eyes

too small to take everything in.

Branches, slack-skinned and ringed,

rise like colossal snouts

to sound alarums. Instead,

bursts of water. Ice

for emphasis. Ricochets

of last night's freeze.

It's as if the morning sun

set the animal heart of this tree

bellowing for warmth.

Tusks of ice sheer off

and the hairless giant shakes free

in a flood of equatorial memory.

from *The Napa Review*, 1985

KELLY CHERRY

The Bright Field

Face sharp and narrow as a pencil,
the shrew is a graffito
in the bright field

Nature is a book,
it has been said,
and perhaps God is its author,
and perhaps not

but every living thing
inscribes itself on land, sea, or air
Even rock, even sun
make a statement

Here, we say, *here*
And we say, *There you are*
and there you are

from *Cave Wall,* 2010

PATRICIA CLARK

Across Barbed Wire

Day when the clouds turn to buttermilk by 2 p.m.,
clouds churned thick and transformed to a yellowish-white,
and whatever twists you follow in country roads,
whatever meanderings take you from the main highway,
bring you to a gate, a house, a porch,
leave you at the white door in the garden, four brick walls,
        a spot to sit.

The horse noses pasture grass until you wave,
brown animal with blazed forehead crunching green
        until a hand lifts,
and the apple set out on the hand's table,
the red fruit offered on a palm,
becomes the call that beckons him,
changes into the invitation winding him
up the meadow's greening slope,
up the blazing hill.

It's mostly ridiculous how much we care,
both silly and not silly that it matters to us
who comes or sits, stays or talks,
who arrives or reclines, remains or speaks,
and yet it does—our muscles the storage places,
        hearts like attics

where dreams rise up on every side,
forests climbing inch by inch like green walls,
and hills show the scary expanses,
escarpments display all the frightening views
we thought we had left,
we hoped were gone.

No matter now.
It is not important today.
If you would not escape from me,
if you would not leave my side,
blazed horse or sweet man or kindly friend,
star-marked horse, man with eyes glittering,
       the friend who calls—

then let me say it,
then I'll pronounce it if you allow,
as the stars whirl around, a comet flares,
as galaxies wheel and a tailed ice-ball goes away
       for fifteen thousand years,
how much it helps me to feed you,
exactly what it means for me to nourish you
with my own outstretched paw,
my own extended, soft-palmed hand.

from *Imagination & Place: An Anthology*,
Imagination & Place Press, 2010

BARBARA CROOKER

The VCCA Fellows Visit
the Holiness Baptist Church, Amherst, Virginia

We are the only light faces in a sea of mahogany, tobacco, almond, and
    this is not
the only way we are different. We've come in late, the choir already
    singing,
swaying to the music, moving in the spirit. "When I was down, Lord,
    when
I was down, Jesus lifted me." And, for a few minutes, we are raised up,
out of our own skepticism and doubts, rising on the swell of their voices.
The singers sit, and we pass the peace, wrapped in thick arms, ample
    bosoms,
and I start to think maybe God is a woman of color, and that She loves
    us,
in spite of our pale selves, so far away from who we should really be.
Parishioners give testimonials, a deacon speaks of his sister, who's "gone
    home,"
and I realize he doesn't mean back to Georgia, but that she's passed over.
I float on this sweet certainty, of a return not to the bland confection
of wispy clouds and angels in nightshirts, but to childhood's kitchen,
a dew-drenched June morning, roses tumbling by the back porch.
The preacher mounts the lectern, tells us he's been up since four
working at his other job, the one that pays the bills, and he delivers
a sermon that lightens the heart, unencumbered by dogma and theology.
For the benediction, we all join hands, visitors and strangers enfolded
in the whole, like raisins in sweet batter. We step through the door

into the stunning sunshine, and our hearts lift out of our chests,

tiny birds flying off to light in the redbuds, to sing and sing and sing.

from *Christianity and Literature*, 2006 and *Line Dance*, Word Press, 2008

DEBORAH CUMMINS

Before It's Too Late

So at last I tell her to come out of the trees,
that I can't believe she's followed me
this time to central Virginia, to these hardwoods
at the edge of a hayfield overlooking a valley,
the Blue Ridge hunkered against the horizon.
Her voice of bitter complaint weaves in and out
of the leaves.

          Before she gets to what-might've-been
had she married a smarter man,
and how of course I'd never understand
with my fatter wallet, my bigger house, I call
Come on, it isn't, as you always insist, too cold.
If the wind musses your hair, that, at least,
is easily fixed.

          And though I never get back
whatever she must've said—or sung perhaps?—
withdrawing from my room, sleep hovering near,
the door ajar, a light in the hall reassuring,
I promise not to invent, again, another mother
who reads the classics or is happy
to walk the beach alone, stay up late with Mozart.
Before it's too late, I tell her

              Come feel
the sun on your face. Watch how wind,
climbing this slope of unmown hay, carves absence.
Let's agree that hawk, looping the thermals,

fools no one it's just on a joy-ride.

Here's a log mapped with lichen

light hasn't touched yet. We can sit

at an easy distance, nothing between us.

from *Counting the Waves*, Word Tech
Communications, 2006

CAROL V. DAVIS

Driving Through Rural Virginia

It's time to talk about differences.
You, the son of a German baker,
born during the war, me,
the daughter of Jews, born after.
Thrust together in rural Virginia,
where we walk streamside as I try
to identify trumpet vine and bull thistle:
the triumph of Blue Ridge wildflowers in spring.

Having left behind all other identities,
the lives we are wedded to on separate
continents, the incompatible languages.
Sometimes I think I would do anything
for stability or resolution, as surely
as now I risk everything.

We drive towards Bedford, past falling fences
and handpainted signs advertising fruit
and you ask if I lost family in the war.
I can tell it is difficult for you and I am amazed
by the fluency of your voice.

There are those I cannot name,
cousins left behind in Vienna
and Cologne, a son sent to Palestine

in what appears a dangerous choice.
Our bible doesn't go back far.
The family name lost on Ellis Island,
first names bastardized through assimilation:
Yitte Chana becomes Edith Ann and so on.

When I let your thick hands run their course
it is in full belief of such ironies.
Even on this splendid day as we wind our way
through an unsuspecting countryside,
ever confident, ever blinded.

from *Hawaii Pacific Review,* 1995 and *It's Time to Talk About...*, Symposium, 1996

CARLA DRYSDALE

New Year's Eve at the Artists' Colony

for David Del Tredici

I loved looking at him.

His head jerked and shook

the trashy yellow shag wig he wore.

He grimaced and shuddered, eyes wild, focused.

A spaghetti strap from his pink nylon slip

rolled down to rest on a ledge of muscle

between his shoulder and triceps.

Music tore through his body

his hands stormed the keys

the piano shrieked in primal notes

we felt in our human bones.

I loved looking at him.

He played for us—the dreamers, creators,

eccentrics, the driven, the insecure,

the arrogant, the labelled and unlabelled,

the disowned and owned again

as the year crested and rolled forward again.

from *Little Venus*, Tightrope Books, 2009

MOIRA EGAN

Hearts & Stones

for Coleman Hough

I have a friend who collects heart-shaped stones.
She plucks them out of nowhere, catching glints
and glimmers of this gift, the earth present-
ing chthonic valentines to her alone.
Of marble, crystal, sandstone, fossil, quartz—
her vast collection spans a glacier's age.
It's said collectors are trying to assuage
a hole within, some awful primal loss.
If that's the case, I want to tell her that
we all have empty spaces, awful scars.
Even the earth accretes itself in layers;
that force creates both precious stones and granite.
And if her heart-shaped stones reflect the one inside,
I want to tell her every heart is petrified.

from *Discovering Genre: Poetry*, Prestwick House, 2006; *Spin*, Entasis Press, 2010; and *Rip the Page! Adventures in Creative Writing*, Shambhala Publications, 2010

GEORGE ELLENBOGEN

Buzzards by a Dead Dog

We pull over by the side of the road,
outside wheels still resting on the pavement
and follow an air full of frost and yelps
to four pups, stubby legged but leaping

at buzzards perched in a sycamore,
used to barking, patient as uncles
we've left over thanksgiving dinner
waiting for their brandy and cigars.

At the center is a dog, freshly dead;
whether hit by an eighteen wheeler
or brought to this gully by mange,
we don't walk down to see which.

She says this is how it ought to happen,
in the cold of the year, with nothing left
to chance, and protest nothing more
than mongrels' yelps. There's not much more to make

of this. Sun blaze turns the snow to glints
that cardinals cut in flight. Nothing here
for elegy. We shift back into first
and penetrate Virginia's afternoon.

from *The Rhino Gate and Other Poems*, Vehicule
Press, 1996 and *Morning Gothic: New and Selected
Poems*, Vehicule Press, 2007

CHARLES FISHMAN

A Field in Virginia

A wide gate swings open . . .
The hip-high grass children hid in
only two days ago has been mown.

Wade through the gold-leafed waves,
the rose-headed clover; walk
the shadowy edge of the field.

Over this river of cut grass
the sparrow hawk circles. The sun
blurs your footsteps in this world.

Walk out again when the sun
burns down the sky and the blue
sharpness of daylight is a white haze

on the hills. That fragrance you breathe
is the heart of the seed split open.
Press firmly on this green earth,

this sea of life you tread on.
Something will spring alive in you
and root down.

from *Pedestal Magazine,* 2003, and *Country of Memory,* Uccelli Press, 2004

ALICE FRIMAN

Eyesore

To the west, Blacks.
To the east and southeast down the bend,
Whites. Between, the old couple—Monacan Indian,
perhaps the last—grazing their skinny cows,
hoeing their patch. The Mister once said, sure
he remembered me, but how *could* he, me coming
maybe five times in twenty years. But for me
he was fixture, made to order—baggy overalls,
grizzled cheek working a wad, Chevy pickup
up on blocks. One rusted geranium.

Now six years later I return—
country road, meadows, the old poplar
shimmying down one more October. My movie,
my pastoral, just waiting for me to walk my walk
and take my place. What didn't hold tight
until I came back? Even that brown dog,
trembling like a lover, showed up each day
to bark his heart out to my empty spot.

*   *   *

There are two kinds of not seeing—
when you can't or when you don't.
If you suffer from the latter, better depend
on shock, immense fallacies, mackerel
falling from the skies, or in this case
an empty yellow school bus careening, hell-

bent around the bend, headed for disaster or,
like a ghost on fire, fleeing one. A patch
spliced from a grade B movie to fill the hole
big as a bus left by what was missing.

The old man, gone—truck, barn,
house, the works. I tramp the empty yard,
trying to conjure up the groaning porch,
the ripped screen door, the annual geranium
anemic in its pot. But light glares.
The movie has let out early. And look.
Nothing but neatness and hush in a plot too flat
for these Virginia hills, and tread marks
running back and forth like a crazed eraser
with purple wildflowers scrambling over it fast
as if they knew what's buried there and would tell you
if they could take the time to stop.

from *Margie*, 2004

BECKY GOULD GIBSON

Summer Solstice in Pastels

for Danny

She leans her notebook against a blue metal gate, tie-dyed with rust.

The yellow pasture she comes to by day is still now,

buff grasses bordered by trees; beyond them, blue mountains.

Is that a cicada whirring or crickets?

What would he use here—ochre? Burnt sienna?

Blue chalk for the bloom sun loves to give metal?

A cow snorts in the distance.

How can light leave so quietly a gate on the first day of summer?

All she ever wanted—easy light, easy relationships.

An hour earlier she sat for a pastel portrait

on the back stoop of a new friend's studio.

As trees lose their outlines slowly, he squints, dabs on more color.

Is it enough to mean blue, to mean yellow?

He signals her to turn her head to the original angle.

The light goes as he paints. He rubs out one eye, does it over.

Field of cows, field of the painting.

Can we ever see anything as it is with the field always changing?

Where does yellow become pink—exactly?

Every evening if she allowed it, she'd feel this unmooring.

A cow at the fence scratches her chin on barbed wire,

sky's blue deepens as fireflies come. The moon brightens, trees dim.

from *Chiron Review*, 2010

L. B. GREEN

Selections from
Of Work and Song on Mt. San Angelo

1.

I've come to the pastures in March. Where soon,
after lunch, the long shadows of trees
and the long tails of the black cows: bond,

brush meadows and fields. Carrying forth the *myths*—

I light a candle, straighten and sweep my room,
for the studio, ramble near and distant hillsides,
search for jasmine's brave and brilliant yellow.

With no luck, and plagued by ladybugs, I grab
the dictionary for something more,

know already the little beetles: dine on aphids
and insects that damage the crops of neighbors,

are *Coccinellidae, named for our Lady, the Virgin
Mary.* Instead of beloved blooms, they fill
the glass bowl on my desk, outer wings

red-orange with circles of black, where piled
in heaps, in mounds, they lie perfectly still.

4.

An anodyne: the pear
you cut, the Anjou, sweet
with green skin and firm flesh.

Ah. Desire. Over and again we conjure,
plumb its meaning. *A simple game of
semantics, for only you can know.*

Each day it curls in you: aware
and unaware. From the starry-lit universe,

you pull a plea that calls the self
front and center, to various

purposes, beyond which may—in brief
time—anoint, provide riches, procure sex,
build you up, cleanse you. Or trigger

impulse: the way one red bromeliad,
on the windowsill, disregards its smallness,
turns toward light, its curing

and necessary rays: when without
sound or recognizable motion grows
into the now, into the picture, into

the future.

6.

Incorruptible body: Bernadette
of Lourdes's face; her hands
holding, through eternity, beads
for us to pass by and see.

We: the foolish, the worldly: stare, marvel
yield to such sights. The drawing:
an oil pastel of two blue

chairs: legs, backs, bottoms unadorned,
and finely drafted. There is little else, light

and dark: his stage, an absolute:
for two, or for no one.

In the kitchen for hot water,
for tea, you bump into someone
you don't know.

Only the wifi man,
he says. Technology
and the mind at work. The mind:
a network. You return to the studio.

To and from the figure you read
while checking for ticks,

which may have attached to your ear,
or arm, or leg and carried back
from your walk across the fields.

Schubert's *Winterreise* resounds
in evening:

Dream of Springtime,
Der Lindenbaum's whisper,
and the *lingering look at a lime tree...*

one whose lament is: unrequited
love, and loneliness: all wrapped

together: agony and exultation:

your mother dying:
...the cycle earth-bound...
...leafbuds again wing-like...

from *Night Garden*, 2009

RALPH GRÜNEBERGER

Old Virginia

for Ronald Horwege

The mills grind slowly
Even in Amherst County.
But with flour there is no money
To be made in a satiated land.

The water pours out of a
Mile-long pipe onto the mill wheel
And sets the cast iron parts from
Indianapolis into motion. While

The man from the Amherst Milling
Company peddles dog leashes, horse saddles,
Cattle drovers and hand-carved
Sticks. A handful of
Nails or a handful of flour
Recognize the difference.

Everything that goes with good bread
Knives & corn, tobacco & tea, beans
& berries, the man sells. According to

The chart of the Dixie Miller Combination
Of 1893 five pounds of wheat grain
Yield three pounds of pure

White flour. What a calculation!

If only I could produce five words

And you would read three from them.

from *The Mystery is: You are and you are not.*
American Poems, Aphaia Verlag, Berlin 1999

KENNETH HART

Women's College

I didn't think of myself as a sex offender
or as someone whose sex was offensive
until I walked across the campus
of the women's college. I tried to be
as inconspicuous as possible, looking away
when someone jogged past with a scrunchy holding back her hair
and breasts bouncing just a little beneath a sports bra,
making believe I had some business there
by putting a purposeful stride in my step.
I know I carry the chromosome of hatchet murderers and rapists,
it's no wonder my hands felt like mallets
at the ends of my arms.
After awhile I sat on a bench
and tried to look at the oval pond,
the trees and manicured shrubbery in front of the study hall,
as passing girls gossiped in the late-January sunlight,
some of them tanned from winter break, or slightly heavier
after a month of their mother's cooking.
So I got up to leave,
making sure my shoulders looked slumped and unathletic,
a little afraid of myself now,
and massively unaware
that one of them might consider my presence
a welcome relief.

from *New Ohio Review*, 2011

NEVA HERRINGTON

Woodchuck at the Art Colony

At dinner someone mentions a sighting,
a resident appearing too often
to discredit, not familiar, bigger
than a rat, chestnut brown, and slow moving.
City folk, most of us, we guess: *Hedgehog?*
Groundhog? Finally *woodchuck* satisfies.

So I'm prepared several days later
for the stir in the field near my door,
the body lumbering through sunlit brush,
a celebrity to transients surprised
by a creature requiring no other
than ground-level horizons, at home here.

from *The Chariton Review,* Spring 2002 and *Her
BMW and Other Poems,* Pudding House
Publications, 2007

CON HILBERRY

Virginia Night

Virginia night with stars, not much to do
but lose the path and watch Orion rise.
Supposed to be a comet passing through.

When sun is up, we feel obliged to hew
some timber, show some enterprise.
Then comes Virginia night, the deepest blue.

One fist of stars is faintly clear when you
look somewhere else—then they vanish, vaporize
like the promised comet that's not passing through.

The dipper spills its emptiness into
my cup. No need. My pitcher's twice that size.
Virginia night and stars, they drink it too.

Solitude and night may help me brew
the juice to freshen memory, what lies
just out of reach, a comet passing through.

Some lovely lives have vanished, one or two,
their shadows on the walk, their arms, their eyes.
The night, the stars, they've done what they can do.
There might still be a comet passing through.

from *Dunes Review*

LORI HORVITZ

Art Colony Birthday Party

I

Last night I played a salad bowl, hand and spoon
slapping rhythm upon a cold steel semi-circle,
tossing clinks and gongs and jangles and tinks
instead of lettuce.

A quiet painter broke into dance, arms flailing,
body squirming, legs joyfully slicing through a sliver-moon sky.
Sweaty and breathless, while searching for lost keys,
the quiet painter learned her father's heart had failed.
Now keys were beside the point.

I think of my mother, whose heart gave out
while I wandered through Pompeii photographing
toga-draped embraces embalmed in plaster white.
But the photos came back black—
the same blackness of the big limousines
rolling out of a New Jersey cemetery
when I finally heard the news.

II

The second a photograph is exposed to light
it begins to fade until whiteness
turns to sky to sand to sea
and aren't we made up of mostly water?

Once I locked eyes with a deer
and all the ships lost in the Bermuda Triangle
sailed between us.

III
Like fireflies needling at the night sky,
we strive to leave our marks.
In the meantime,
we can dance and paint,
drum on salad bowls,
honor our mothers and fathers
and the startled women of Pompeii
huddled together
in a last mummified embrace.

from *Facets Magazine*, 2002

COLETTE INEZ

Witness to a Meadow in Virginia

Cows kneel in fields
fireflies have abandoned.
Soon another year of flickering,
a comet's shower of flowers in the grass.

I was born in another country,
Leopold, the cruel king.
I embroidered butterflies
on handkerchiefs

sold by the African missions.
A child, I said *papillon*,
and fluttered my wrists,
imagining shiny coins in boxes

shipped to the Congo
where children dreamed
severed hands of their ancestors
took wing on the path.

Today I bow to the swallowtails,
spangled fritillaries and sulphurs
as if they were royalty.

from *Neo*, 2006

MARGARET B. INGRAHAM

Proverbs

Does not wisdom call,
And understanding lift up her voice?
On top of the heights beside the way,
Where the paths meet, she takes her stand.

Proverbs 8:1-2

Yesterday was clear
and warmer than we would expect
this time of year
on the lip of Blue Ridge.
Bull bellowed through the afternoon
and the little dipper
tipped a glimmer from beneath
the gauze of stratus curtain
blowing in.

By morning clouds had settled
and an odd mockingbird came quietly
to sip remnants of rain
from the cement planter
out beside corncrib,
and all four of them—

cloud, bird, stained water, concrete box—
carried the same inference
of gray.

Although I waited all day
for the familiarity of winter
shadows dropping long, falling dark,
before they would finally recede,
nothing moved across the field
except the breeze,
nothing met me on the path
except westerly wind turning in
at dusk.

I know that night will show itself
this way along the high ridge
of Mt. San Angelo:
pillar of cloud will dissolve
into the gray solitude of cattle
sighing and that mysterious wisdom
we came here to know
will slip invisibly inside
silence's fence.

from *Nimrod International Journal*, 2006, and *Proper Words for Birds*, Finishing Line Press, 2009

HALVARD JOHNSON

Old Virginia Trees

Here's one called "Only Our Chagrin Remains"
standing alone in the middle of a cow pasture, forsaken
by its leaves, left starkly branched against a partly clouded sky.
Another called "Liberation of the Mind" hunches
over the road to the highway, dropping its late fruit
on passersby. A nearby copse cries out, "Come!
Join us! We, united, shall prevail!"

Our refusal does not stop there. It is insatiable
and knows no bounds. Our leader, thinking beyond
the limits of time and space, says, "At the hour
in which I write, new tremors fill the air above the field.
We must be brave enough to face them." His collected works
wave from his branches like tiny hands. His name,
we think, is "Poverty is Not a Crime."

"The hand that writes," he says, "is worth the hand
that ploughs." And we all say, "Amen." Our revolutionary
will is strong in us. We wish the transformation
of the world to be as radical as it can be. On this mental
slope, the mirrors of inconstancy do not disturb us.
What, indeed could they expect of us? Everything leads us
to the belief that "The Last Days of March" will be our savior.

from *Organ Harvest with Entrance of Clones*,
Hamilton Stone Editions, 2007

MARILYN KALLET

Ode to the Open Window
(Sweet Briar)

Like Archimedes' glass
you prove air,

blue hills,
scent of boxwood.

You let me glimpse
kingly cardinals

who rock the feeder,
peasant sparrows,

woodpeckers
on their state visit

to spring seed.
In turn they open my

childhood, hints
of my father,

gone twenty years.
I toss them cookie crumbs

and the birds bring news
of him, generous one

who left secret chocolates
and sent me Yuban

in grad school.
The feeder swings

like a scale with
the past pumping it,

Daddy weighs in
light, incorporeal,

a good man, scared man,
who loved me.

And Mom?
Not part of the bird show.

She turns up at public events,
award ceremonies,

in prize gardens,
when I'm handling money.

She watches over Heather
at Northwestern,

always craved ivy.
March, and the sash

stays open, though
when I have the chance to view

Mother in the casket,
I say: not this time.

After the funeral pageant
she had ordered fire,

though some deemed cremation
scandalous for a Jew.

Stylized,
she may have been worried

about how she would look
in her bones.

One can forgive ashes,
leave violets

by the headstone.
Sunlight and sprouting earth

prove the here-and-now
as spirits float through you.

from *Packing Light: New and Selected Poems*, Black
Widow Press, 2009

LUANN KEENER-MIKENAS

Sweet Briar Colony, the Lovers

Late afternoon, the lovers go by my window
following the dirt road between fields
of wild grass ripening in June sun.
Their darker and lighter heads gleam
bronze, flaxen, before shadows take them,
the sweating green lawn, the bowery trees.
Once a mansion stood here, once,
the giant copper beech, alive now
almost three centuries, bore its full crown
of blood-dark leaves. Fire and lightening
sundered these. The mansion's ghost,
peaceful and beneficent,
hovers over the artists' residence.
The copper beech lives on with half its glory.
Seen from the south, it still looks whole.
This solitary pair have come
from separate marriages to try
their fate. I know they're not just
walking toward eternity—they're going
for an afternoon swim. Come on, heart,
skip the melancholia. Still, watching,
the breath catches underneath a rib. What may
become of them? The oldest story,
full of briars sweet and bitter, pungent oils

love draws from skin the sun is slowly aging—
like the bronzing grasses in these tumbled fields
where the world both is and isn't
real. Where each night at their open window
the lost moon, falling, tips its grail.

from *Quarterly West*, 1992

SYBIL KOLLAR

The Cows (Sweet Briar)

In this twilight I miss the cows
although they've been gone for years.
The winding mud road is reassuring
even though it leads to the empty barn
where I used to hear their stirrings
and watch them galumph out to pasture, their
mouths breathing the fire of cold mornings.

I first met them in a field late at night while
I was chewing on an imported mushroom
and after they began their slow walk
toward me, it was their huge eyes that seemed
to detach and float, their bodies left to wander.

Lately all that matters is what's missing:
my dead uncle reciting from "Rhyme of the
Ancient Mariner" as he drilled my teeth,
my lucky nickel, the last blue antelope.

Twilight moves into night its streaks
of red and amber flow through the ghostly trail
of their haunting eyes like shining stars long dead.

from *New Millennium Writings*, 2004

ANGELA KREUZ

eternal moment

we went for a walk

me and my shadow

following the path which went up the hill

listening to the concert of crickets

passing twisted trees, an osage orange,

I bent forward and touched the lime-green fruit

never seen such a funny thing

like a brain of an alien,

gave it to a horse

horsey didn't think about it, I guess, just ate it

the rails blinking in the sun

all shades of green, red and yellow around us

the sky—blue—with a cirrostratus

me in the floating world

diving into the eternal moment of time

uns auf schwingen, Gedok, 2010

LAURIE KUTCHINS

Summerless

The lake is so cold the man from Bavaria
is the only one who swims in it and only
because he is practicing for the northern
bay water of the Pacific. Late,
in the field, a handful of lightning bugs.
Too chilled to flit about, they huddle
in the grass, morse-coding a calculated
message to the kidnapped summer.
What could their fires change, brief
as a girl's love for a gaudy ring found
by its shine in the bottom silt? Snuffed
green lanterns, powerless
heat asleep in the wings.
yet they are what haunts me
as the summer passes.

from *Poetry*, 1996 and *The Night Path*, BOA
Editions, 1997

TERESA LEO

Virginia Farm Haunting

In memory of Sarah Hannah

Just when I thought I could take it,
put it away,

find some esophageal strength
to swallow it down,

her scarred image breaks through—
it can't just rest

in the trachea, the back of the throat,
it has to rear up and swoop down

the way the hawk after last night's rain
intended to grasp something running in the field,

but the field I see is charred and black;
even the cows are missing,

maybe loaded into trucks
to herd and wander elsewhere.

I'm left at this window in the barn
to watch the imperceptible blades

trying to push through again,
but know they'll only get so far,

not even to the surface, let alone
to the compound's wooden gate.

What tree could honor her?
Catalpa, dogwood, maple—

none could rise up far enough
to reach what's left

of the dark, dark sky.
At home I could plant flowers,

perennials that double their presence
by coming back year after year,

gathering force in winter
to break spring's hard ground.

But I'm here, the place
where we first met,

and I look perhaps too closely
at each mockingbird or blue-tailed skink,

the dragonfly that hovers
at the picnic table

as briefly as a slap across the face
brings blood beneath the skin

to one place, then retreats
without a trace. Suddenly

the field is green again,
the cows back at the fence.

Tonight, I'll wait by the gazebo for her
long after everyone goes to sleep.

Each tree makes its futile attempt,
in every turning leaf I hear her name.

from *The Country Dog Review*, 2010

GINNY MACKENZIE

No Leash Law

I approach a white house.
Despite being astigmatic, I see
a fence—electric,
two barking dogs inside:
the large one, mostly Lab,
exits a gate. I need
to pass this house
to arrive at the field
where the sun sets. Our need
for beauty overcomes caution.
I never make eye contact
with beasts. Still, when
I'm halfway past the house,
the big dog growls at my side,
baring teeth whiter than bone.
I put my writing hand in my pocket.

The next day I learn
there is no leash law
in Sweet Briar. I pick up dog
mace called *Halt*
and a large club from many provided
in dumpsters and head up
Old Stage Road
the opposite way, where
the only vicious dog

is said to be a brown and white
bull dog at the 4th house—but
after a series of biting incidents,
sources tell me that dog
is *no mo.* I'm hopeful
this is a euphemism
for dead. For two days,
my luck holds out. I fall
into lassitude. On the third day,
I see a barking brown
and white fur muscle
approaching. No one is around.
I have no choice but to proceed. I
don't have my *Halt*
or my club. I curse myself
for not having my cell phone. Then I hear

a male voice, loud but with such
a Southern drawl, I have no clue
to the content. A big man
is holding out his hand—palm facing me—
like a crossing guard.
Don't move, he says.
I think, oh he must be kidding.
I yell, *Does that dog bite?*
But he repeats the hand signal—
only more emphatically.
Don't move, he says, and he's running
after the dog which is getting
closer to me but misses him.
He picks up a rock

and throws it.
The muscle is hit and yelping.
It runs toward the white house.
I hear a man say a woman

needs to go past. Now, the man
is standing in front of me—
his hand out, this time for a handshake.
I take his hand. It's sweaty.
I'm Dave, he says. He has a serious stutter
and a serious drawl.
Glad to meet you, I say.
Does that dog bite, I ask.
Yes, he does, he says.
Thinking I can't be hearing right,
I speak loudly and slowly.
I even use sign language.
Does that dog bite? I ask
and make my right hand
into a mouth of teeth
and grab my left arm with it.
Yes, he does, he says again.
Now I'm really upset.
The next time you see this dog, he says.
Stop. Don't move. You understand?
O.K. Dave, I say and stumble
back onto the blacktop.

from *Prairie Schooner*, 2007

MARY MACKEY

from *Lynchburg*

. . . the Confederate boys made themselves
into grass
and the Yankee boys made themselves
into gravel roads
they made themselves into cold fronts
coming in from the north
and tornadoes
sweeping across from the west
and hurricanes blowing in
from the Gulf
and sycamores
and pines
and red dirt

and the widows of the boys
made themselves
into wild onions
plantain
and dandelions
stumps of old trees
fields of hay
and red gashes in the grass where
the new bypass
is coming through
into kudzu

and clover
white rocks
brick buildings
and small windows
with neat wooden frames
libraries
and spent hunting shells
black cows loose on the road
and they're still remaking themselves
moment by moment
into empty beer cans
and girls with long hair
and trucks carrying packages
and propane

the mules that hauled the cannons
made themselves into creeks
and hot asphalt
and the horses the officers rode
made themselves into railroads
and dogs
churches
and broken plumbing
and rust
and they keep on remaking themselves
like the ragweed
and wild roses
that line the ditches
along Coldwell Road

the birds are
relearning their songs
from moment to moment
the kernels of corn
the leaves of the tobacco plants
the mud in the river
have no duration

on that June day in 1864
when the ones in gray rode in on the train
from Charlottesville
and the ones in blue walked over the rise
everything around them
was dying and being reborn

so the boys
took aim
and made
each other
into deer ticks
and mice
the sweet center
of common white clover
dust on windows
in the stables where
the wealthy girls keep
their horses
distant thunder

crows

and a woman in a green T-shirt

bending down

to pick an armful

of flowers

from *Breaking the Fever*, Marsh Hawk Press, 2006

ELIZABETH SEYDEL MORGAN

The Place You Left

I'm leaning again in my doorway
here in the sun that is merely the place
where the sun used to be.

The silence is surfaced by usual noise—
woodpecker in Ollie's pasture,
the Norfolk & Southern's morning clatter.

The emptiness is spotted with objects
you will remember: dome of blue sky,
fat bees, pink rock holding open the door.

There are still some things to touch—
a sculpted egg, thistle pods, my cheek
against my fingertips.

Instead of dog, walnut, lemon,
there's more lilac now.
But even that sweetness is just a place
where lilac used to be.

from *The Governor of Desire*, Louisiana State
University Press, 1993

TANURE OJAIDE

At Mt. San Angelo, outside the real world

On this early dawn walk, I stop before the real world begins.
Crossing over would be insane, and I retreat to consort
with rabbits, squirrels, bluebirds, blue jays and a pageant
of spring flowers that make the garden of Mt. San Angelo.
I will live outside the real world for as long as I can do so.
Authentic beauty goes uncorrupted by competing fads—
no resident tampers with the divine craftsman's sculpted
image of each; all follow the diurnal rhythm of the mount.
Outside the real world, I live to the full my incredible dreams.
"Within Mt. San Angelo, nobody's been sick," says a composer
who survived a holocaust and traveled golden decades here.
Really there are no doctors, only cooks and servers.
Last night's full moon is entering the trench of daylight.
Peace holds here, with no wars to fund or rigged elections
to contest. Over the mountain girded by ravines, outside
this haven, politicians of all cultures lie for a living.
I won't give up this mountain for another residence
out there recovering from the shock of mass murder.
Here I am not afraid of my tall shadow; no amber alerts.
I will not cross over to the real world this early dawn
for all the dollars and made-up faces out there to chase.
O Aridon, keep me out of the real world for this ecstasy,
the primeval garden of love on this mountain residence

from *The Beauty I Have Seen: A Trilogy,* Malthouse
Press, 2010

KATHLEEN O'TOOLE

Winter of Ice and Straw

1.

So little evergreen, in these hills

so few bursts of pine fir to break

the mute browns of mud and bark, grass straw

yellow, and the weathered grey of shed

and barn, fences.

Morning illumination:

a quarter-mile stretch of barbed-wire, molded

overnight into a line of icicles around so many fists

of rust. Backlit with sunrise, such clarity

sculpts a tension of opposites, reprises

a tribulation in these Virginia mountains;

sunshine shredding itself

on the hundred tiny spikes of thorn bush

branching back skyward.

2.

In a cemetery in Tubberpatrick, Ireland, a century-old oak wears the prayers of the countryside—strips of rag tied onto the long-dead native hardwood. Worn from memory now, the name of the saint who's said to have hallowed the tree, even the healings granted. But it's known all around that the ground consecrates the remains of their hanged heroes, and how the local farmers dragged the bodies to midnight burial, matted with straw and blood, fields away from the barn where their cornered lives were ground out.

3.

At nightfall here
       it's the 'black ice'
on the roads that kills.

       Frozen patches of invisible script
signing curves and hollows with epitaphs—
       illegible until they're interpreted
by speeding tires
            already
out of control.

4.

The crossings are iced up the highway where a young mother figures her chances. A wager she's making this winter, not fully knowing the road. Nights for studies and dreaming awake while the boys slumber. Beat the clock, armed with as much schoolwork as she can cram between shifts, the rides to fetch children, and the weary hours. It's a schedule etched in her bones (not hers alone) told to spin straw into independence, up that mountain slope. Quick, before the slow thaw drives hundreds like her into the one lane cleared for passage.

5.

Which birds are scavenging

the underbrush and hedges and what

do they require to survive

                    until spring?

Watch the dipping flight of bright cardinal

pairs dodging each other for boxwood

cover. A clatter of blue jays tap at iced maples

as if gauging sap flow. Just how much

bounty is burrowed in a landscape

so thoroughly stripped

            that the wind's shrill note

etches only blackbirds dipping toward night

            plaintive as a scarecrow's shadow ?

6.

Today's full color photo above the fold: an Afghan family making bread of grass, their final hedge against famine. Grinding dried grass in winter on the stone face of war—salt water for binding what remains into a crust. What tree could elevate such tattered strands of prayer toward Mecca? Raw hands and hollow eyes. Silence willing straw to flour. Head scarves lift with the snow-edged mountain winds.

from *Meanwhile*, David Roberts Books, 2011

LIA PURPURA

Era

Once there was a love for words hitched, shotgun—

blam to *hagiography*,

anarchy to *smack* and many ersatz

dislocations,

reckless mentions, referrals abounding.

I'd like to know what all along didn't care

so I can sidle up,

and there lay down

in all its muted musicality,

its hum and color

just a tint now, pausing,

curling over the realest wreckage.

Out back, four phone wires cross the yards.

Trees balance their green leaf notes there.

Under breath.

After the day is fine-sifted

it waits.

It waits to be taken away and grows

meanwhile

beautiful and unseen.

Meanwhile the day takes its time.

Any thought in the language of trees

is one side silver, one side green.

Having rained last night and
shimmering off,

the day is turning briefly hot again.
Some birds out there sound like tigers.

Before I break off questioning

about this one cloud in the soft
watery blue, blue

noted for its company-keeping
year after year,

save the odes that water it down,
blue so large

it's an ease and a breath,

I'm seeing how it serves

for robes,

for ceilings,
is a patient model

for smaller imitations of itself.

from *Indiana Review*, Anniversary Issue, 2003.

KIM ROBERTS

Darwin in Reverse

Faith carries its own bedroll.
I'm on the lookout for a saint
even though "there are no motels
for a man of God," and the standard for macho
is driving without using your blinkers.
"You just send in your check and the next day

new gorillas have been discovered"
knuckling sidewalks, asking you for more.
They want your life: fortune cookie,
tea leaves, the lines of your palms.
But "after you've seen a man
running around in his briefs

it's hard to call him maestro,"
pander your lowercase ambitions,
scratch his itch. He loses
that manicured continent quality,

deflates to country, then county,

acre, square foot, and finally

inseam measurement.

from *The Wishbone Galaxy*, Washington Writer's
Publishing House, 1994

STEVE ROBERTS

Knowledge of Cows

Cows stand still like a picture.
Some chew. Some move. Last winter,
The rocks you threw didn't puncture
The frozen pond. Now even air ripples
Its surface. When we went to sleep, cows
Stood by the fence. When we woke up, cows
Still stood by the fence. You talked to them.
They did, or did not, respond. Fallen leaves
Rattle, rise up to branches. More rattle,
Fail to raise themselves to wood. Would
You remember the front porch shrub's
First spring sprout? Shadows line the ground
Where robins search for worms. A pair
Of leaves stuck in fence wire, more swirl
Into the pond. Dried dung turns to dirt.
A snake's hole found by scattered feathers,
Light finds me inside my room. The sun lowers
Behind the spruce to signal the cows' return.

from *A Space Inside A Space*, St. Andrews Press,
1999

JENNIFER ROSE

Mt. San Angelo Postcard

Virginia

Cicadas here work overtime, three shifts

of buzzsaws building some imaginary highrise.

A primal rooster crows, lackadaisical

about the hour like good vacationers.

Ailanthus wears its sporrans, as if dressed

for some parade, and the corn has put its aigrets on.

One mockingbird trades songs like baseball cards.

Underfoot, a million crickets hiccup.

Two cows chew clover daintily, quaint ladies

out for salad and a tête-à-tête.

Blue mountains loom abroad, the muses' Ararat.

At night the fireflies' lights, flickering

like half-remembered words, decorate

the lawn's elaborate garden party. A few birds

sing late, most lyric after all the garden's guests have gone,

while the moon watches, accidentally left on.

from *Hometown for an Hour*, Ohio University Press, 2006

THADDEUS RUTKOWSKI

Leaping Buck Icons

I see deer walking the yard,
in sunlight, one at a time,
leaving the screen of trees
for the glare of snow,
stopping to graze or listen.

Hours later, they appear again,
walking in the other direction,
nose to tail, a small herd,
responding to a coming storm.

Inside the art colony house,
insulated from the frightful weather,
someone complains about her editor,
someone else lies folded like a fetus,
someone else elbows the piano keys.

Out on the highways,
at the approaches to natural pathways,
diamond-shaped road signs
with silhouettes of leaping bucks
warn, "Caution. Deer crossing."

Inside, we are too concerned
with the potentiality of language,
the hunger of the word,
and gap-filled, light-filled discourse
to care about mere deer.

from *Mobius: The Poetry Magazine*, 2006

NEIL SHEPARD

This Is How It Is

Sweet Briar, Virginia

I'm old enough to know this daylight
savings time's a ruse, yet I'm out here
near sundown, haunting one more hour
of light, inhaling flowers like there's no
tomorrow: lilacs, especially lilacs,
that incarnate bait: open your mouth
waft this in, now tell me you don't want a body.
And there's more where that came from: bleeding
heart, marsh marigold, blossom of plum and persimmon,
all floating in spring ether. I'm out here, suckered
by spring and this heart—what to do but smother it
in flowers, daylight savings flowers that come
long before the first gold hues of leaves,
longer still before inexorable green
spoils my mood. Green says I'm growing
old and mute as moss. In April rain, May
swell, June fulcrum, July slide, August dust,
I hear it. And September, September's leaves
hang like dog-eared pages I'd rather not read
again. Oh, for October where together we tear
to shreds those stories of second-comings, watch
them fall down around us. The older I grow,
the closer in age to god, who is timeless.
Soon I'll be going home. Today, I'm burying my face
in flowers, trying to smell from the living side

what it'll be like when I'm swimming
in flowers, and I don't smell a thing.

from *This Far from the Source,* Mid-List Press,
2006 and *Poetry Daily,* 2006

ENID SHOMER

Among the Cows

Advised to breathe with the Holsteins
    as a form of meditation,
I open a window in my
    mind and let their vast humid breath,
sticky flanks, the mantric switching
    of their tails drift through. I lie down
with them while they crop the weedy
    mansions, my breasts muffled like the
snouts of foxes run to ground. I
    need to comfort the cows, the way
heart patients stroke cats and the grief
    of childhood is shed for dogs. I
offer them fans of grass under
    a sky whose grey may be the hide
of some huge browser with sun and
    moon for wayward eyes. It begins

to rain. How they sway, their heavy
    necks lift and strain. Then, like patches
of night glimpsed through a bank of clouds,
    they move toward four o'clock, the dark
fragrant stalls where dawn will break first
    as the curved pink rim of their lips.
I want to believe I could live
    this close to the earth, could move with
a languor so resolute it

passes for will, my heart riding

low in my body, not this flag

in my chest snapped by the lightest

breeze. Now my breath escapes with theirs

like doused flames or a prayer made

visible: May our gender bear

us gracefully through in these cumbrous frames.

from *This Close To The Earth*, University of
Arkansas Press, 1992

TAIJE SILVERMAN

On Joy

Last night's rain has filled the fields
with cornflowers, blue-bright as moons
in children's books, all milky light.
They seem, my father says, *the kind of color
that could show up in the night.*

Cornflowers wilt in heat.
By noon the sun will burn the fields
green, as if no bloom had known them.
I picked one to keep, and now
it's the color of paper. My mother's sick.
Today begins her twenty-second day of radiation.
As I write she is strapped to a table
under fourteen floors, face held to a net
of white while instants of light like lead move
through her. I don't know how to say it.

Past these fields are others no one sees,
and past them oak and poplar trees, the evergreen
that slopes up toward a mountain range the same
blue shade and lucid gleam as these quick blooms.
Last night, rain fell in flooded streams.
I tried to wait, but dinner starts at six and by the time
I'd reached the house my dress was slick.
I didn't rush. The drops were warm
and made me laugh, out loud—the laughter's sound

familiar and strange, the way that sometimes
when we listen, breath is strange.
As if our loneliness were something I could speak,
when even crickets know we only speak to air.
I want to ask the air, then, how a love
so skilled at longing can become
enough. Why do prayers to no one comfort us?
I want so much. I want a faith I've not
invented, something hard, uncontested as our yard's
wooden table, something that won't ever sound
like my name. Now the afternoon's late.
Light sharpens the skyline like glass in a lens,
making mountains look bluer against where they end.
This light must come from nowhere.

Last night, I walked to dinner on a gravel road
through rain into a joy so unaccountable
and plain, it did not need a witness. But walking back,
the rain had lifted. And in its place, mist drifted low:
a thousand-fingered ghost that seemed to coax
each leaf and blade into a long, inhaled wait,
though what arrival they awaited had already left.
I stopped to watch, but wept.
We've moved for months through hospitals,
learned every name for star-shaped cells
doctors cut from my mother's brain and stained
onto slides before calling us into an office.
Maybe we don't bear the unbearable. Maybe
we die with it. And in our place some larger,
less impatient shape may then be granted space
but I don't want it. I want my mother.

Sometimes beside her in the bed while trying
to tell her I'm okay, I start to weep.
She watches me. Her eyes are distant now,
gone deep inside some gravely gentle place
where, with a stranger's curiosity, she seems ask
What can I do with your sadness? She has no use for it.
We will lose what we love, and our suffering
is useless, and by dusk all the crickets will thrum
their one absence of warning. That trace of light
against the hills will spread through trees, undo
the ends of evergreen, then fall to fields. It will not hold.
As if it means to urge us, *look*. Love's body must
be manifold. Black cricket shell, new summer air,
late light. The landscape's all ablaze
with gentle strangers. *Look*. We're standing in a field.

from *Ploughshares*, Spring 2008 and *Houses Are Fields*, Louisiana State University Press, 2009

MELISSA STEIN

Anaphylaxis

The wasp there again when I surfaced:
those dangling legs, the budlike head,

lethal black thorax drilling
inches from my lake-clogged ear.

I dove beneath and swam, again,
to the limits of my breath, through

the bath-warm surface, through
cold current. Out of our element,

what other story is there—pursued,
pursuer, panic in the long strokes?

The death that insect carried
was not the one I wanted. And oh,

I wanted death, or thought I did: days spent
twitching a razor at my wrists,

cuddling a little mortuary of pills
in my palm. Yet when it came

I swam from it as any prey.

There was still something left to want.

from *Rough Honey,* American Poetry Review, 2010, winner of the 2010 APR/Honickman First Book Prize

ELISABETH STEVENS

Swimming to the Dam

The day I swam to the dam,
I didn't want to drown,
I wanted to say good-bye.

Alone in the opaque pond,
trees bent over its banks
like green angels,

I was weighted down
as though carrying your body
in my arms.

I made it the whole way,
touched the moss-shrouded wall,
let the water take everything.

I turned,
saw an enormous weed
growing beside the sluiceway.

With a quick breath,
I started back,
light and easy.

A long way, but
I was not tired.
Almost there,

sure of myself,
I called back,
"Good-bye, good-bye."

From the sluiceway,
came the echo,
"Good-bye, good...bye...."

from *The Night Lover, Art & Poetry*, Birch Brook
Press, 1995

STEPHEN TAPSCOTT

Mud

It is early in the history of the season of humid freshness, herbs, and mud.
I walk across the sod of the meadow, which is after rain a bitter sponge.

I am almost afraid to see how weighty I feel to the earth, which has
       suffered me this long time
and still supports me, imprinted with corresponding scars.

Many things I have thought and felt I am not proud of and are best not
       talked about, disgracing the body:
not even with God, who knows them as acts, having witnessed,

and who does not after all demand to be told them as a condition of
       forgiveness.
Therefore I print them here, setting my feet carefully where my body
       touches

the softer body of the meadow—as if to make them more exact,
a condition of the dark receptive soil:

as if prayer were a specific longing, as if the forgiveness I pray toward
would be a specific forgiveness and I will know it when it comes.

from *From the Book of Changes*, Carnegie-Mellon
University Press, 2002

ALICE TEMPLETON

Song Beside the Barn Wall

Culture me, if it can be done. Make me a letter
to stand beside other letters, a stone to fill
the proud wall's gap. And if I fit, build
the wall sturdy, a fast and true anchor to trim
this reeling world. Wind me a path, one among many,
rising so subtly that higher seems flat, the ordinary level
of what lies ahead. Distance me, deepen me, deem me
a number, a blank of time in all its tenses,
a loosely woven sum where sense can come and go:
sweet tea of the cut lawn, salty beach of noon
in your hair. When the last step tips the wits
of my inclination, when memory shakes open its prize,
when all the division in my body gives itself up,
stay with me, letter to letter, stone against stone,
day among days, then and now absently weaving
patchwork from the fresh cut grass: my finest burlap,
my first thread, my loom beside the old barn wall.

from *Poetry,* 2003

VIVIAN TETER

Notes on Hunger at the Artists' Colony

December 2007, Virginia Center
for the Creative Arts

Always something Christ's sake to feed

or water even this

whoever heard of keys needing

humidity naïve writer placed in composer's

studio just fill the can okay

just slip the black nipple would you

over the mouth of the clear tube

yes on hands and knees

under the grand you're given

all this and asked one task so feed

the water slowly into the mystery

of how what the fingers place

into the mouth day after day burns

to notes of praise free

of the body's clank and drag

sweet praise-notes rising.

from *Virginia Wesleyan Review*, 2010

J. C. TODD

Spring Ephemerals

Breath, sweat, the dust
and flake of flesh
tinge petal, leaf, mold

on the edge of fetid. Our trace
in a bank of wildflowers.
Scent rising

from what we've crushed
clears the sludgy mind.
We're losing sense of ground,

loosening our sense of what's
properly human.
Such profusion. Bluebell,

cohosh, Dutchman's breeches—
we'll be among them
for almost a month.

From the treads of light
hikers kicked off
in the mud room

the fragrance of their dying
underlies our coming in,
our going out.

from *What Space This Body*, Wind Publications, 2008

ALISON TOWNSEND

Reading the Famous Woman Poet's New Book, also about Persephone, on First Day of Spring

I see her point, of course, about hell
being a kind of perpetual winter, an Antarctica
of the heart it pains Persephone to leave,
a place where nothing flourishes but the bitter taste
of these chopped-off lines, this grim interpretation
the famous poet defines as *candor*. But there is more
than one way of telling the truth. And I can't help
but believe in something else as I stare into the old
apple tree opening outside my window this first day
of Blue Ridge Mountain spring, where forsythia erupts
in yellow fountains, azaleas shake out ruffled silk
skirts, and narcissi have been up been up for weeks,
each blossom a cup of scent it seems almost possible
to drink. No leaves on the trees yet; that's true.
But as I walked by the lake last night I could feel
it coming, all the edges of my body dissolving
for a moment as I touched a catkin spilling
from a branch whose name I did not know, the tiny
chartreuse explosion attached so delicately it broke
beneath my hand. *Surely this is the way to live,*
I thought, in pursuit of some kind of mercy,
believing green will come again, even when it departs,
falling to earth, leaving us guilty for keeping one leaf
from what it might have been. And perhaps it's naive
or romantic, but this morning, gazing into the apple,

trying to mark exactly where pink turns into white

(as if seven drops of blood had been stirred into

a pail of milk to paint the outer shells of each petal),

I surrender to the idea of return, to the belief

that people, places, things do come back, happy

to be here—even if we cannot see them the way

I see this flowering apple, or the way we want, even

if changed from what they were—the war between winter

and being alive the oldest one there is—a honey-scented

insurrection, a pyre of white fire these open petals

resurrect, as I lean toward them, trying to transcribe

again the great and ordinary mystery of being mortal.

from *Persephone in America*, Southern Illinois
University Press, 2009

MARTIN TUCKER

On Leaving an Artists' Colony

Collecting things:
haircuts at five dollars a throw,
so cheap I am going to bring back two of them,
but this is froth at the top of a list
I've lathered for the month I'm here.

A soapbar I recycle for memory's brush,
the smile of dogs barking a morning run,
swimming across the lake in a raft of afternoons,
and wires of wheat bailing out a violet sky.
Or, atop a pink construct an artist built in on the green,
I view New River Valley's sun splatter all day.

So many things to put in order:
the trees I leave contain an essence of me
that, contrary-wise, is nowhere missing for my going forth.
The frame in which I have sat for thirty days
will no longer shape my natural shades.
But this is what I am taking:
touch of soil in the cutting of a sunflower,
like a haircut purchased ahead of its time,
and the explosion of a tendril growing.

from *Attention Spans*, Confrontation Press, 1997

MEMYE CURTIS TUCKER

Rubato

Tonight, the virtuoso
is taking liberties. His fingers slur,
almost forget. Yet the audience responds

to the sudden pianissimos, slow releases,
the thin body leaning into crescendos,
and Liszt's master trick—robbing

some notes, lingering on the ones he loves.
He's left behind the certain, dependable rhythms:
grandfather clock deep in the nights of childhood,

the beat of his first metronome before its
broken weight began to slide, sleeping-
cars ticking the miles between concerts.

He gazes past the audience, gathering
the times he has touched these phrases, playing now
in counterpoint to memory.

from *The Watchers*, Ohio University Press, 1998

G. C. WALDREP

Tropic of Cancer

What one finds threatening another finds organic,
even comfortable, two bars in 4/4 time taped
against a bedroom window; transparent in the same way
the skin is, light penetrating to a certain depth then stopping,
suddenly, as at a root definition. A primary color:
red, yellow. What vacancy will unite this sequence?
Outside stars scrape against the night's file with a precision
we've mapped onto the surface of memory,
Once there was a forest, and we were in it.
Once a man with a sword held a woman's head.
There must have been a tune to go with that, a rhythmic cry.
Still the alphabet evinces a tranquility,
all human endeavor abstracted into a finite
number of strokes, the kind of game a child invents
in a moment of boredom, ad hoc. And teaches to friends
his own age. By bedtime he'll have forgotten the rules....
Tell me a story. But the names sleep gives us
have all died from the tongue, syllables caught
between tooth and lip at the moment of waking.
At some point the music assumes an orthogonal suspension,
one player on each floor in a space projected ever upwards.
Does this affect the tuning? Does the Doppler
draw the vertical? And when, precisely,
does the performance end?—Reluctant aseity

twice repeated, first the hard consonant, then the soft.
The spirit of God moved upon those waters.
One wants to believe, yes. One wants in fact
to think of vowels so holy their notation is unnecessary,
a common faith, something to scroll in sand
and ashes while the mind blanks and the hand
moves lightly across a brushed surface. You reach out,
touch the media, feel that faint thrum.
I sing of arms and a man. We begin to remember!
Those that go down to the sea in ships....
But the musicians, tired, have long since descended and dispersed.
A single note is heard. As if from a great distance.
I steady the prow of your bones, make you feel normal.
There's a splinter of glass in your pale eye.

from *Goldbeater's Skin*, Center for Literary
Publishing, 2003

BJ WARD

Upon Being Told Again There Are No Rhymes
For Certain Words

Crossing to my studio eighty yards
through some briars, I lug a verbal freight:
both volumes of the New Shorter Oxford
English Dictionary. I contemplate
a carpenter bringing a lumber pile
to his wood shop—I want to build structures
from words that readers could live in awhile.
I know it's rare, tricky stuff, such scripture—
umpteen poets, still no rhymes for purple.
Bonds could beat McGuire and Ruth—but orange?
I'd reconstruct Heaven, or usurp Hell—
write till I swing open like a door hinge.
I arrive—a guest who'd refurbish town.
I take my pen, begin to nail things down.

from *Gravedigger's Birthday*, North Atlantic Books, 2002

MARJORY WENTWORTH

Stillborn

Blue jays zigzag through leafless
black branches at the edge of
the winter field where a cow
has lain for three straight days, since
birthing a stillborn calf.
When she moans, the cry comes from
the great gulf of grief that is
motherhood. One tree trembling,
alone; red berries on tips
of the tallest branches,
this is what the cow sees
through air, the color of tears.

from *The Southern Women's Review*, 2010 and *The Endless Repetition of an Ordinary Miracle*, Press 53, 2010

MICHELE WOLF

Night Vision

Mt. San Angelo

We venture beyond the gold
Sockets of light, into the murky
Blackness, each footfall
A crunch on the gravel drive,
A path we have memorized.
Under a sky slurry with cloud, no
Stars, our shadows, elongated
Flat Giacomettis hand in hand,
Stilt-walk ahead of us, sink
Headfirst into the night's
Opaque pool. Colors
Fade into sharpened sounds:
Constant mower-shrill cicadas
Drown out the dark, lost green
Of the dewy grass. Past
The curved stand of trees,
The moon, pearly and round, greets
Us like a sudden spotlight, gilding
Our outlines, posing as backdrop
For our ripened silhouettes.
My eyes, adjusting, blink,
Absorb the beams of your gray
Eyes: black, two orbs of the night
Lighting a trail that will lead

To the lake, still, obsidian shiny,

Edged by the long-stemmed antenna

Heads of monochromatic

Wildflowers. Silent,

They watch us while

We stare at each other,

Our bridged, wavering image

On the water, pale and indistinct.

from *Hubbub*, 1991; *Keeper of Light, Painted Bride Quarterly*, 1995; and *Conversations During Sleep*, Anhinga Press, 1998, winner of the Anhinga Prize for Poetry

CONTRIBUTORS' NOTES
AND COMMENTS

MARCIA ALDRICH was born in Allentown, Pennsylvania. She teaches creative writing at Michigan State University. She is the author of *Girl Rearing*, published by W. W. Norton and part of the Barnes and Noble Discover New Writers Series. She has had essays appear in *The Best American Essays*, *The Beacon Book of Essays by Contemporary American Women*, and a wide range of literary magazines. She is the editor of *Fourth Genre: Explorations in Nonfiction*.

KARREN LaLONDE ALENIER was born in Cheverly, Maryland. She is the author of five collections of poetry, including *Looking for Divine Transportation*, winner of the 2002 Towson University Prize for Literature. Her poetry and fiction have been published in such magazines as: the *Mississippi Review*, *Jewish Currents*, and *Poet Lore*. *Gertrude Stein Invents a Jump Early On*, her jazz opera with composer William Banfield and Encompass New Opera Theatre artistic director Nancy Rhodes premiered at New York City's Symphony Space Leonard Nimoy Thalia Theater in June 2005. Composer John Supko is collaborating with her on *How Many Midnights*, an opera about Jane and Paul Bowles. She writes for *Scene4 Magazine* at scene4.com.

ANNETTE ALLEN was born in Sioux City, Iowa, and awarded her M.A. from Southern Methodist University and the Ph.D. from the University of Texas. Allen now teaches as Professor of Humanities in the Ph.D. Program at the University of Louisville. The former Dean of Salem College, where she directed Creative Writing, she is the author of two collections of poetry, *Country of Light* (1996) and *What Vanishes* (2006), and essays on Virginia Woolf, Molly Peacock, and Mary Oliver. Among her poetry honors are the Witte Award for her first poetry collection and three state arts council fellowships in addition to the International Residency in Germany awarded by VCCA. Her recent edited book, *Clinical Ethics and the Necessity of Stories*, was published by Springer in December 2010.

REBECCA BAGGETT was born in Wilmington, North Carolina. Her award-winning chapbook, *God Puts on the Body of a Deer*, was published in 2010 by Main Street Rag. Her other collections are *Still Life with Children* and *Rebecca Baggett: Greatest Hits*, both from Pudding House Publications. Her poem, "Alleluia," included in *God Puts on the Body of a Deer*, won Atlanta Review's 2010 International Poetry Competition. Her poems, short stories, and essays have appeared in many journals and anthologies, including *New England Review*, *North American Review*, *Utne Reader*, *Ms.*, *Poetry East*, and *The Sun*. Recent work appears in *Atlanta Review*, *Poetry East*, and *Calyx Journal*.

NED BALBO was born in Mineola, New York. He is the author of three books. *The Trials of Edgar Poe and Other Poems* (Story Line Press/WCU Poetry Center) was awarded the 2010 Donald Justice Prize. *Lives of the Sleepers* (University of Notre Dame Press, 2005), received the Ernest Sandeen Poetry Prize and a ForeWord Book of the Year Award. His first book, *Galileo's Banquet* (Washington Writers' Publishing House, 1998), was awarded the Towson University Prize. *Something Must Happen*, a poetry chapbook, appeared from Finishing Line Press in 2009. The recipient of three Maryland Arts Council grants, he has received the Robert Frost Foundation Poetry Award and the John Guyon Literary Nonfiction Prize. "My Father's Music," an essay on adoptive identity and ethnicity, appears in Creative Nonfiction's anthology of Italian-American prose, *Our Roots Are Deep with Passion* (Other Press, 2006). A poetry fellow at the Sewanee Writers' Conference, the West Chester University Poetry Conference, and the Virginia Center for the Creative Arts, he has published poems in *Able Muse*, *Antioch Review*, *The Dark Horse*, *The Hopkins Review*, *Notre Dame Review*, *River Styx*, *Sewanee Theological Review*, *Shenandoah*, and elsewhere. A Long Island native, he teaches at Loyola University Maryland and lives in Baltimore with his wife, poet-essayist Jane Satterfield, and her daughter Catherine.

"The Minor Hours," Balbo's poem evoking VCCA, is a text requested by and written especially for composer Donald Hagar. The text was published by Sibelius Music; the piece was performed by the Brooklyn Conservatory Chorale at the Lafayette Avenue Presbyterian Church and the Brooklyn Conservatory Concert Hall in June 2009.

KAREN BELL was born in Brooklyn, New York. A photographer and book artist, she has photographed the environment for many years in all phases of existence: in full blush of beauty and shortly after major disasters. In every effort she has sought the particular beauty, the hope, the future of what she was seeing.

Bell earned an M.F.A in photography from Rhode Island School of Design and has taught and lectured on photography and video at numerous institutions. She has been on the faculty at The New School, teaching photography for 16 years. In 2005 she started teaching photography workshops at the Brooklyn Botanic Garden. Fellowships include Yaddo and the Virginia Center for the Creative Arts, where she currently holds the position of Chair of the Fellows Council. Bell has received grants from Women in the Arts for video editing, and from The New

School to create a video about two unsung photographers. Bell's photographs and artist books are in the collection of the Brooklyn Museum, New York Public Library, and Ellis Island Museum of Immigration, among many other public and private collections. Her photographs, hand-made books and videos have been exhibited throughout the United States, Australia and Israel.

MARY BONINA was born in Worcester, Massachusetts. Her poetry, fiction, and memoir have appeared in *Salamander, Hanging Loose, Gulf Stream, Istanbul Literary Review*, in many other journals and in several anthologies, including *Voices of the City* from Rutgers University Center for Ethnicity, Culture and Modern Experience (Hanging Loose Press, 2004). Her most recent collections, *Clear Eye Tea* (2010) and *Living Proof* (2007), were published by Cervena Barva Press. She is also the author of *Lunch in Chinatown*, a chapbook of poems inspired by the experience of teaching recent immigrants English language classes in their work places. Her memoir, *My Father's Eyes*, has been excerpted in many journals and was first alternate for the VCCA Goldfarb Fellowship (2002) and received Honorable Mention in the University of New Orleans Study Abroad Contest (2009). As winner of *Boston Contemporary Authors* competition, a public art project, her poem "Drift" was etched in a granite monolith permanently installed outside a busy Boston subway station. In addition to being a Fellow of the Virginia Center for the Creative Arts, Bonina has also been awarded a Vermont Studio Center fellowship. She holds an M.F.A. from the Program for Writers at Warren Wilson College.

ANDREA CARTER BROWN was born in Paterson, New Jersey. Her first full-length collection, *The Disheveled Bed*, was published by CavanKerry Press in 2006. Previously, her chapbook, *Brook & Rainbow*, won the 2000 Sow's Ear Chapbook Competition and was published in 2001. For the past five years she has been working on a book-length poem titled *September 12*. Poems from this manuscript have won the 2011 James Dickey Prize from *Five Points*. Previously, an heroic double sonnet crown from *September 12* won the *River Styx* International Poetry Prize. A selection of poems from this manuscript, *Each Boat Signs the Water,* won the 2010 Pudding House Chapbook Competition and will be published in 2011, together with a letterpress broadside of the title poem. She lives in Los Angeles.

About "Blues, For Bill," Brown writes, "This poem was begun during my second residency at VCCA in the late 1990's. The previous fall, my mentor, and friend, William Matthews, had died suddenly. Although almost a year had passed, I was still coming to grips with the enormous hole his death left. While at VCCA, I was thinking about him a lot. In his collection, *Blues If You Want*, is a poem I have always especially loved, 'Mood Indigo', which draws on memories of time spent on a dairy farm in Ohio. The presence of the cows on Mt. San Angelo made this poem very present to me, making it in turn possible for me to write my own homage to Bill under the spell and in the spirit of its lyrical mystery. When 'Blues, For Bill' was finished, for the first time I felt I had done justice to him for all he had given me, and I will forever be grateful to VCCA for giving me that poem."

ANDREA HOLLANDER BUDY was born in Berlin, Germany. She is the editor of *When She Named Fire: An Anthology of Contemporary Poetry by American Women* (Autumn House, 2009) and the author of three full-length poetry collections: *Woman in the Painting* (Autumn House, 2006), *The Other Life* (Story Line Press, 2001), and *House Without a Dreamer* (Story Line Press, 1993), which won the Nicholas Roerich Poetry Prize. Other honors include the D. H. Lawrence Fellowship, a Pushcart Prize for prose memoir, the *Runes* Poetry Award, two poetry fellowships from the National Endowment for the Arts, and two from the Arkansas Arts Council. Her poems and essays have appeared in numerous anthologies, college textbooks, and literary journals. Since 1991 she has been the Writer-in-Residence at Lyon College, where she was awarded the Lamar Williamson Prize for Excellence in Teaching. "Writing Studio" was written in W-10 during a summer residency in 2009.

FRAN CASTAN was born in Brooklyn, New York. This poem was written during a stay at VCCA in 1982. Castan's latest book, *Venice: City That Paints Itself*, has just been published by Canio's Editons of Sag Harbor, New York. This collection of her poems and her husband Lewis Zacks' paintings was created during two extended stays in Venice while living and working in a community of artists and later refined over the following decade. *The Widow's Quilt*, an earlier collection of Castan's poems, with an introduction by William Matthews, has won praise from Robert Bly, Robin Morgan, Bruce Weigl and Florence Howe, among others. It contains several prize-winning poems, including "Operation Crazy Horse," winner of the Poetry Society of America's Lucille Medwick Award. Castan taught writing and literature at The School of Visual Arts in Manhattan for 25 years.

KELLY CHERRY was born in Baton Rouge, Louisiana, and grew up in Richmond, Virginia, where her parents started and played in the Richmond String Quartet and her father co-founded the Richmond Symphony. She is the author of twenty books of which the most recent are *The Woman Who* (stories), *The Retreats of Thought* (poems), and *Girl in a Library: On Women Writers & the Writing Life* (essay and memoir). She is Eudora Welty Professor Emerita of English and Evjue-Bascom Professor Emerita in the Humanities at the University of Wisconsin in Madison. Her numerous awards include the Hanes Prize for Poetry, the Bradley Lifetime Achievement Award, a USIS Speaker Grant to the Philippines, the Dictionary of Literary Biography Award for best book of short fiction, fellowships from the NEA and the Rockefeller Foundation, and publication in the prize anthologies *Best American Short Stories*, *Prize Stories: The O. Henry Awards*, *The Pushcart Prize*, and *New Stories from the South*. She is a member of the Electorate of Poets Corner at the Cathedral Church of St. John in New York. In 2010 she was a Director's Visitor at the Institute for Advanced Study in Princeton. She lives in Virginia and is the current Poet Laureate of the Commonwealth of Virginia.

PATRICIA CLARK was born in Tacoma, Washington. She is the author of three books of poems, most recently *She Walks Into the Sea* (Michigan State University Press, 2009) and also *My Father on a Bicycle* (2005) and *North of Wondering* (1999). She also co-edited an anthology of women writers, *Worlds in Their Words*, with Marilyn Kallet. Clark teaches creative writing at Grand Valley State University in Michigan where she is also the university's poet in residence. Her work has appeared in *The Atlantic Monthly*, *Poetry*, *Slate*, *Stand*, *The Gettysburg Review*, and many other literary journals, including online at *The Huffington Post*, *Poetry Daily*, *Verse Daily*, and *Terrain.org*. She has received The Mississippi Review Poetry Prize, an award from the Poetry Society of America, a grant from ArtServe Michigan, and placed second in the Pablo Neruda Competition from *Nimrod International Journal*.

BARBARA CROOKER was born in Cold Spring, New York, and is the author of three books of poetry: *Radiance*, winner of the 2005 Word Press First Book Award and finalist for the 2006 Paterson Poetry Prize; *Line Dance* (Word Press, 2008), winner of the 2009 Paterson Award for Excellence in Literature; and *More* (C&R Press, 2010). Her writing has received a number of awards, including the 2004 WB Yeats Society of New York Award (Grace Schulman, judge), the 2003 Thomas Merton Poetry of the Sacred Award (Stanley Kunitz, judge), and three Pennsylvania Council on the Arts Creative Writing Fellowships. Her work appears in a variety of literary journals and anthologies, including *Good Poems for Hard Times* (Garrison Keillor, editor, Viking Penguin) and the *Bedford Introduction to Literature*. She has been a Fellow at VCCA fourteen times since 1990, and is the full-time caregiver for her adult son with autism.

DEBORAH CUMMINS was born in Chicago, Illinois. She is the author of two full-length poetry collections, *Beyond the Reach* and *Counting the Waves,* as well as a poetry chapbook, *From The Road It Looks Like Paradise*. Her poems have been featured on Garrison Keillor's *The Writer's Almanac* on NPR, in the *American Life in Poetry* newspaper series edited by former U.S. Poet Laureate Ted Kooser, and in various journals including *The Yale Review, The New England Review, Shenandoah* and *Orion*. The winner of numerous awards and fellowships, she also serves on the board of the Poetry Foundation for which she was board chair during its transition to a private operating foundation. She and her husband reside in Evanston, IL and Deer Isle, ME.

CAROL V. DAVIS was born in Berkeley, California. She won the 2007 T.S. Eliot Prize for *Into the Arms of Pushkin: Poems of St. Petersburg* (Truman State University Press, 2007). Twice a Fulbright scholar in Russia, she was the 2008 poet-in-residence at Olivet College, Michigan, and teaches at Santa Monica College, California. Her poetry has been read on NPR radio and on Radio Russia. Her other books are *It's Time to Talk About...* (bilingual Russian/English, 1996), and two chapbooks, *Letters From Prague* and *The Violin Teacher*. Her new book, *Between Storms*, is forthcoming from TSUP in 2012.

Of this poem, Davis writes: "My residency at VCCA in 1993 was a godsend, coming two years after the birth of my third child. During that three week period at VCCA, I wrote 20 poems, which formed a section of my first full-length collection, *It's Time to Talk About...*Each of the poems in that section begins with the line, "It's time to talk about," as does this poem. In previous stays at VCCA, I'd never explored the surrounding area, but this time I did, thanks to another Fellow with a car. This poem is about that day."

CARLA DRYSDALE was born in London, Ontario. Her first book of poems, *Little Venus*, was published by Toronto's Tightrope Books in 2009. Her poems have appeared in Canadian and US journals including *LIT, The Same, Global City Review, The Literary Review of Canada, Canadian Literature* and *The Fiddlehead*. She lives near Geneva, Switzerland, with her husband and two sons.

MOIRA EGAN was born in Baltimore, Maryland. She is extremely grateful, both to VCCA and to the Mid Atlantic Arts Foundation, for the month she was able to spend at VCCA, during which much of her second full-length collection, *Spin* (Entasis Press, 2010), was completed. Each day, it seemed, some conversation or some interesting experience led to another poem that needed to be written, such as the poem here, which was very much inspired by a fellow Fellow. Further, two of the sonnets written that summer appeared in the *Best American Poetry 2008*. Moira has since moved to Rome, where, with her husband, Damiano Abeni, she translates back and forth between English and Italian. Translations published in Italy include collections by John Ashbery, John Barth, Mark Strand, and Josephine Tey, with more forthcoming. Currently she teaches English and Creative Writing at John Cabot University in Rome.

GEORGE ELLENBOGEN was born in Montreal, Canada. His work has appeared in several collections of poetry and in numerous anthologies and magazines as well as in French and German translations. He has read his poetry on both sides of the Atlantic and is the subject of a documentary film, "George Ellenbogen: Canadian Poet in America."

CHARLES FISHMAN was born in Oceanside, New York. He is Emeritus Distinguished Professor of English and Humanities at Farmingdale State College, where he created the Visiting Writers Program in 1979 and the Distinguished Speakers Program in 2001. He has been editor of the Water Mark Poets of North America Book Award, associate editor of *The Drunken Boat*, and poetry editor of *Gaia*, *Cistercian Studies Quarterly*, the *Journal of Genocide Research*, and *New Works Review*. Fishman has also served as poetry consultant to the U.S. Holocaust Memorial Museum, in Washington, DC, since 1995, and is currently poetry editor of *Prism: An Interdisciplinary Journal for Holocaust Educators*. His books include *Country of Memory* (Uccelli Press, 2004); *Chopin's Piano* (2006) and *Blood to Remember: American Poets on the Holocaust* (2007), both from Time Being Books; *Water under Water* (2009) and *In the Language of Women* (2011), both from Casa de Snapdragon, LLC; and *The Death Mazurka* (Texas Tech University Press), a 1989 American Library Association "Outstanding Book of the Year" that was nominated for the 1990 Pulitzer Prize for Poetry. *Country of Memory*, *Chopin's Piano*, and *Water under Water* all received the Paterson Award for Literary Excellence.

ALICE FRIMAN was born in New York, New York. Her new collection, *Vinculum*, is from LSU. Her last two books are *The Book of the Rotten Daughter* and *Zoo*, winner of the Ezra Pound Prize for Poetry from Truman State University. Her work appears in *The Southern Review*, *Shenandoah*, *The Gettysburg Review*, *The Georgia Review*, and *Best American Poetry 2009*. She is Poet-in-Residence at Georgia College & State University in Milledgeville, Georgia.

BECKY GOULD GIBSON was born in Greenville, South Carolina. She has published two prize-winning chapbooks of poetry and three full-length collections, *First Life* (Emrys Press, 1997), *Need-Fire* (2005 Poetry Book Competition, Bright Hill Press, 2007), and *Aphrodite's Daughter* (2006 X. J. Kennedy Prize, Texas Review Press, 2007). *Need-Fire* received the 2008 Brockman-Campbell Award given by the North Carolina Poetry Society for the best book by a North Carolina poet in 2007. Her poems have appeared in numerous journals, among them, *The Hiram Poetry Review*, *Brooklyn Review*, *Comstock Review*, *Iris*, *Kalliope*, and *Feminist Studies*; as well as in several anthologies, most recently, *Don't Leave Hungry: Fifty Years of Southern Poetry Review* (2009). Her awards include a North Carolina Arts Council Literary Fellowship in Poetry (1993) and a nomination for the Twentieth Annual Pushcart Prize in Poetry (1995). Gibson has just begun her second term as mentor to young poets in North Carolina Poetry Society's Gilbert-Chappell Distinguished Poet Reading Series.

L. B. GREEN was born in Paul's Valley, Oklahoma. She is the author of *Judas Trees North of the House* (2003), *Night Garden* (2009) and *THE ART OF SEEING In Sweet Silent Thought* (2010), a collection of poetry and photography. The North Carolina Arts Council, the MacDowell Colony, and the Virginia Center for the Creative Arts have awarded her grants and fellowships in literature for poetry. Freelance writer, poet and painter she has also been the recipient of both the Robert Ruark Foundation Prize and the Randall Jarrell Prize for poetry. Her paintings and drawings have been shown in regional and national solo and group exhibitions. She lives and works in Davidson, North Carolina.

RALPH GRÜNEBERGER was born in Leipzig, Germany. He studied from 1978-1982 at the Institute of Literature in Leipzig. He writes poetry, prose, and texts for children, monographs, literary criticism, and since 2007, has been editor of the series "new poetry book." Several of his publications were created in collaboration with visual artists and photographers. Since 1996, Grüneberger has been Chairman of the Society for Contemporary Poetry and, since 2000, he has been a member of the German PEN Center. He has been honored with many prizes, including the "Menant Prize for Erotic Poetry" and the "Irseer Pegasus," and he has participated at poetry festivals in Corfu, Paris, and Struga. His poems have appeared in English, Croatian, Dutch, Russian, and Polish. In 1997, 1999, and 2001, he was a Fellow at the Virginia Center for the Creative Arts. A new edition of *The American Poems: The Mystery: You are and you are not* was published in 1999 and will appear shortly with a recent American poetry supplement.

BERNARD (Bernie) HANDZEL was born in Poland. At the age of eleven, his family moved to New York. His interest in art and science started early. He went on to study art and science in college and printmaking in graduate school. Handzel's love of photography began in childhood. He recalls his father taking family photos with a Soviet copy of a Leica 35mm camera. In the 1970's, Handzel began to photograph and worked as a freelance assistant to professional photographers, eventually starting his own business specializing in architectural and still life photography. He writes, "During my 30 years in this field, I've had many wonderful photo experiences, an outstanding one being time spent at VCCA."

KENNETH HART was born in Newark, New Jersey. He teaches writing at New York University, and works in the family roofing business. Recent poems and reviews have appeared in *Mead: A Journal of Literature and Libations*, *F Street*, *Journal of New Jersey Poets*, and *New Ohio Review*, where "Women's College" was published. Hart's book, *UH OH TIME*, was the winner of the 2007 Anhinga Prize. He lives in Long Valley, NJ and Anchorage, AK. "Women's College" refers to Sweet Briar College.

NEVA HERRINGTON was born in New London, Connecticut, and lives in Alexandria, Virginia. She is the author of *Blue Stone and Other Poems* (Still Point Press, 1986) and a chapbook, *Her BMW and Other Poems*, from Pudding House Publications.

CON (Conrad) HILBERRY was born in Illinois. He grew up in Ferndale, Michigan, studied at Oberlin College and the University of Wisconsin, and taught literature and creative writing at DePauw University and Kalamazoo College. His book, *Luke Karamazov*, is based on interviews with the convicted murderer, Larry Ranes. Hilberry has published a half dozen books of poems. The most recent are *After-Music* (Wayne State University Press, 2008) and *This Awkward Art* (Mayapple Press, 2009), which pairs his poems with those of his daughter, Jane Hilberry.

LORI HORVITZ was born in Decatur, Illinois. Her short stories, poetry, and personal essays have appeared in a variety of literary journals and anthologies including *The Southeast Review*, *Hotel Amerika*, *Thirteenth Moon*, *Dos Passos Review*, *Quarter After Eight* and *P.S.: What I Didn't Say: Unsent Letters to Our Female Friends* (Seal Press). She has been awarded writing fellowships from The Ragdale Foundation, Yaddo, Cottages at Hedgebrook, Virginia Center for the Creative Arts and Blue Mountain Center. A former New Yorker, Horvitz now makes her home in North Carolina, where she is an Associate Professor of Literature and Language at UNC-Asheville.

COLETTE INEZ, born in Brussels, Belgium, immigrated to the U.S. at age eight. She has since authored eleven books of poetry, has been widely published and anthologized, and has read her work in colleges and universities, nationwide. Her earliest, *The Woman Who Loved Worms* from Doubleday & Company, won the Great Lakes Colleges National First Book Award. Her last title *Spinoza Doesn't Come Here Anymore* was released by Melville House Books in 2004. It was followed by her memoir, *The Secret of M. Dulong* from The University of Wisconsin Press, in 2005. Her latest collection *Horseplay*, from Word Press, appeared in late 2010. Among her many honors are fellowships from the Guggenheim and Rockefeller Foundations, two awards by the National Endowment for the Arts, two Pushcart Prizes and several awards from the Poetry Society of America on whose governing board she has served. Currently on the faculty of Columbia University's Undergraduate Writing Program, she also taught at Ohio, Cornell, Bucknell, Colgate and Denison Universities, The New School, Hunter and Kalamazoo Colleges, and has instructed at writers conferences, conducted poetry seminars, and appeared on public radio and TV. She reports of her residencies here: "VCCA has given me a haven of calm and beauty in which to write poems and memoir prose. I am forever grateful for that generosity. This poem was obviously inspired by several stays at VCCA."

MARGARET B. (Peggy) INGRAHAM was born in Atlanta, Georgia. She is the recipient of an Academy of American Poets Award, the 2006 Sam Ragan Award and several fellowships from VCCA. Her poems have appeared in over 75 national and international print and online journals. Her chapbook *Proper Words for Birds* (Finishing Line Press) was nominated for a 2010 Library of Virginia Award. Her *This Holy Alphabet* (Paraclete Press, 2009) are adaptations based on her translation from the Hebrew.

About "Proverbs" Ingraham writes, "I 'met' Hilary Tham during my first VCCA residency when I opened the desk drawer in W3 to find her welcoming note for the next Fellow. A few months later back in Washington I was invited to a small dinner in her honor. We connected immediately. It was the beginning of a deep, but far too short, friendship. In February 2006, the day before I departed for another VCCA residency, I visited Hilary in the hospital. The previous summer she had been diagnosed with lung cancer. Hilary had been scheduled for a residency herself a few weeks later, and as I left she said, 'Tell Sheila I won't make it this year.' I'd see Hilary again before her death, but we both knew she would never get back to VCCA. So when I arrived at VCCA, I dialogued with Hilary in my head, wanting her to know what the days were like. 'Proverbs' was my letter to her."

HALVARD JOHNSON was born in Newburgh, New York, and grew up in New York City and the Hudson Valley. He has received grants from the National Endowment for the Arts, the Maryland State Arts Council, and Baltimore City Arts. He has lived and taught in Chicago, Illinois; El Paso, Texas; Cayey, Puerto Rico; Washington, D.C.; Baltimore, Maryland; and New York City. For many years, he taught overseas in the European and Far East Divisions of the University of Maryland, mostly in Germany and Japan. He has enjoyed several residencies at VCCA, during one of which he met his wife, the prize-winning writer and visual artist Lynda Schor. They currently live in San Miguel de Allende, Guanajuato, Mexico.

MARILYN KALLET was born in Montgomery, Alabama. She is the author of 15 books, including *Packing Light: New and Selected Poems* (Black Widow Press, 2009) and translations of Paul Eluard's Last Love Poems (*Derniers poèmes d'amour.*) Many of her books were written at VCCA. She is the director of the creative writing program at the University of Tennessee, and holds a Lindsay Young Professorship. She also teaches poetry workshops for VCCA in Auvillar, France.

LUANN KEENER-MIKENAS received her M.F.A. in creative writing from the University of Arkansas-Fayetteville in 1986 and won a 1990 Virginia Prize in Poetry. *Color Documentary* appeared from Calyx Books in 1994. She has published poems in many journals including *Poetry, Shenandoah, Quarterly West, Chelsea, New Orleans Review,* and others. Her numerous awards include the Writers at Work First Prize for Poetry from *Quarterly West,* the *Chelsea* 1st Place Award for Poetry, the Mary Roberts Rinehart 1st Place Award for Poetry, and the *Americas Review* 1st Prize for Poetry. She is the recipient of a MacDowell Colony Fellowship and many fellowships at Virginia Center for the Creative Arts. Her poetry has been increasingly concerned with the environmental crisis and the remaking and spiritualization of our relationship with the natural world. A second collection, *Homeland,* is currently circulating. Keener has also written a series of children's poems, "Healing Songs for Children," for dramatic performance in therapeutic and educational settings. Originally from Ector, Texas, she taught English at Virginia Tech for several years before making a career change. She has worked intensively with emotionally disturbed children in residential treatment. Currently she is a therapist in private practice and at Randolph College in Virginia.

SYBIL KOLLAR's poetry collection *Water Speaking to Stone* was published by Pivot Press. Her work has appeared in numerous literary journals including *The American Voice, Chelsea, Columbia: A Journal of Literature and Art, Big Bridge, The Hamilton Stone Review, The Literary Review, New Millennium Writing,* and *Rattapallax.* Her poems have been published in anthologies including *A Formal Feeling Comes: Poems in Form by Contemporary Women,* and she's written poems as text for a song cycle "Just Us" composed for mezzo-soprano and flute by Donna Kelly Eastman which was performed in Washington and was included in the CD Series of the Society of Composers, Inc. She is a recipient of a New York Foundation for the Arts Fellowship/Poetry and is presently working on a prose poem collection *Where the Sticks Fall.*

ANGELA KREUZ was born in Ingolstadt, Germany. She studied philosophy and psychology at Lake Constance and works part time as a psychologist in Regensburg, where she lives. She writes short-stories, novellas, novels and poems. Her first book was *Der Engländer und weitere kurzgefasste Geschichten,* followed by her volume of poetry *lyrische städtereisen.* In 2005 her novella *Scarlattis Wintergarten* was published. A few audio books of her work followed. Kreuz' first novel *Warunee* was released 2007, her second novel *WAAhnsinnszeiten* in April 2009. Her short-story *Schick mir doch ein Mail!* is collected in the textbook *Allerlei zum Lesen for American students* (second edition) by Houghton Mifflin, edited by Herman and Lovette Teichert. She won three literature prizes, Daniil Pashkoff Prize 2010, WertFrei in 2008 and the Limerick-Wettbewerb in 2007. From 2000 to 2003 she was co-editor of the literary journal *Wandler.* Her poems and short stories have been translated into English, Czech and Romanian and were published in various anthologies and literature journals e.g. *poet[mag],* *The Poetry Mill* (Ireland) and *Contrafort* (Moldova). Kreuz is a member of the German Writers' Association, the GEDOK and Autorinnenvereinigung.

LAURIE KUTCHINS was born in Casper, Wyoming. She has published three books of poems, numerous essays, and teaches poetry at James Madison University.

TERESA LEO was born in Carbondale, Pennsylvania. She is the author of a book of poems, *The Halo Rule* (Elixir Press, 2008), winner of the Elixir Press Editors' Prize. Her poetry and essays have appeared in *The American Poetry Review, Poetry, Ploughshares, Women's Review of Books, New Orleans Review, Barrow Street, The Florida Review, Painted Bride Quarterly, Poetry Daily, Verse Daily, Mooring Against the Tide: Writing Fiction and Poetry* (Prentice Hall, 2005), the anthology *Whatever It Takes: Women on Women's Sport* (Farrar, Straus and Giroux, 1999), and elsewhere. She has been a resident at the Virginia Center for the Creative Arts, the Blue Mountain Center, and the Vermont Studio Center, and has received fellowships from the Pew Fellowships in the Arts, the Leeway Foundation, and the Pennsylvania Council on the Arts. She works at the University of Pennsylvania.

GINNY MACKENZIE was born in Clearfield, Pennsylvania. Her manuscript, *Skipstone*, won the Backwaters Poetry Contest and was published by Backwaters Press. Her poems, creative nonfiction and short stories have appeared in *New Letters, Ploughshares, Agni Review, Boulevard, The Nation, Pequod, Threepenny Review, Poetry East, Mississippi Review, Shenandoah, American Literary Review* and *Prairie Schooner*. She won the John Guyon Literary Nonfiction Award and the Ann Arbor Festival Short Story Award. Her short story manuscript was a finalist in the University of Alabama's national fiction contest and was partially published in the anthology of finalists, *Tartts Three*. She has poems forthcoming in the *Southern Humanities Review*, the *Connecticut Review*, the *Antioch Review* and *Hunger Mountain*.

MARY MACKEY was born in Indianapolis, Indiana. She graduated *magna cum laude* from Harvard and received her Ph.D. in Comparative Literature from the University of Michigan. During her twenties, she lived in the rain forests of Costa Rica. Her published works include five collections of poetry, including *Breaking the Fever* (Marsh Hawk Press, 2006). *Sugar Zone*, her sixth collection, will be published by Marsh Hawk in Fall 2011. Mackey's poems have been praised by Wendell Berry, Jane Hirshfield, Dennis Nurkse, Ron Hansen, Dennis Schmitz, and Marge Piercy for their beauty, precision, originality, and extraordinary range. She is also the author of twelve novels including *The Widow's War* (Berkley Books, 2009), the story of a female abolitionist who fights with the first African American troops to fight in the Civil War. Mackey's works have been translated into twelve foreign languages including Japanese, Hebrew, Russian, Greek, and Finnish. For the last twenty years she has been traveling to Brazil with her husband, Angus Wright, who writes about land reform and environmental issues. At present she is working on a series of poems inspired by the works of Brazilian poets and novelists. Combining Portuguese and English, she creates poems that use Portuguese as incantation to evoke the lyrical space that lies at the conjunction between Portuguese and English.

ELIZABETH SEYDEL MORGAN was born in Atlanta, Georgia. With Louisiana State University Press, she has published four books of poetry—*Parties*, *The Governor of Desire*, *On Long Mountain* and, in 2007, *Without a Philosophy*. Her poems have appeared in *Shenandoah*, *Five Points*, *Prairie Schooner*, *The Iowa Review*, *Southern Review*, *Georgia Review*, *Virginia Quarterly Review*, *Bennington Review*, and *Poetry*.

TANURE OJAIDE, a Fellow in Writing of the University of Iowa, was educated at the University of Ibadan, where he received a bachelor's degree in English, and at Syracuse University, where he received both M.A. in Creative Writing and Ph.D. in English. He has published sixteen collections of poetry, two collections of short stories, a memoir, three novels, and scholarly work. His literary awards include the Commonwealth Poetry Prize for the Africa Region (1987), the All-Africa Okigbo Prize for Poetry (1988, 1997), the BBC Arts and Africa Poetry Award (1988), and the Association of Nigerian Authors Poetry Award (1988, 1994, and 2003). Ojaide taught for many years at The University of Maiduguri (Nigeria), and is currently The Frank Porter Graham Professor of Africana Studies at The University of North Carolina at Charlotte. He received a National Endowment for the Humanities fellowship in 1999, a Fulbright Senior Scholar Award in 2002/2003, and The University of North Carolina's First Citizens Bank Scholar Medal Award for 2005.

KATHLEEN O'TOOLE was born in Wilmington, Delaware. She has combined an over thirty year professional life in community organizing with teaching and writing. Her poems have appeared in dozens of publications including *America*, *Christian Century*, *Little Patuxent Review*, *Natural Bridge*, *Poetry*, and *Prairie Schooner* and online in *Beltway* and *Delaware Poetry Review*. Her chapbook *Practice* was published by Finishing Line Press in 2005, and *Meanwhile*, her first full-length collection, in 2011 by David Robert Books. Her 2002 residency at VCCA birthed early versions of the manuscripts, and both the Virginia hills, and the formal restlessness she experienced there are ghost presences in the work.

LIA PURPURA was born in New York. Her recent books include *On Looking* (essays, Sarabande Books), a Finalist for the National Book Critics Circle Award, and *King Baby* (poems, Alice James Books), winner of the Beatrice Hawley Award. Her awards include the AWP Award in Nonfiction, the Ohio State University Press Award in Poetry, NEA and Fulbright Fellowships, three Pushcart prizes, and work in *Best American Essays, 2011*. Recent work appears in *Agni, Field, The*

Georgia Review, Orion, The New Republic, The New Yorker, and elsewhere. She is Writer in Residence at Loyola University, Baltimore, Maryland, and teaches in the Rainier Writing Workshop M.F.A. Program.

Of this poem, Purpura writes, "What made VCCA special for me was not just the time it allowed, but the species of time: utterly rare reverie. This form of time can actually change the composition of my work, allow it to meander and distend and conjecture (the spacious lines and unfilled spaces in "Era" are unusual for me). This poem went on a good roam and wasn't restless. It maintained its sense of being destinationless for a long while. VCCA and its wide open range does a spectacular job of gathering in those of us suffering regimentations and salving us with a dose of bygone, as I said, reverie."

KIM ROBERTS was born in Charlotte, North Carolina. She is the author of three books of poems, most recently *Animal Magnetism* (Pearl Editions, 2011), winner of the Pearl Poetry Prize. She is editor of the online journal *Beltway Poetry Quarterly* and the print anthology *Full Moon on K Street: Poems About Washington, DC* (Plan B Press, 2010). She has been a resident at VCCA three times.

Of this poem, Roberts writes, "The epigraph is from an essay on contemporary gardening books in the *New York Times Book Review*, July 22, 1991. A number of lines were taken (out of context) from fellow residents at the Virginia Center for the Creative Arts. Lines 3-4 are from Star Black, on Jimmy Swaggart. Lines 8-9 are from Linda Heller, on environmental mail solicitation. Lines 13-15 are from Daron Hagen, on Leonard Bernstein.

STEVE ROBERTS was born in Wilkes-Barre, Pennsylvania. He is the author of two full-length collections of poems, *Another Word for Home*, Main Street Rag Press, 2010, and *A Space Inside A Space*, St. Andrews College Press, 1999, and also of a chapbook, *Every September. . .*, Tragically Hip Press, 1998. He is the recipient of a 2010 North Carolina Arts Council Regional Artist Project Grant, and was a presenter on the "Art and Healing" panel at the 2009 North Carolina National Alliance for the Mentally Ill (NAMI-NC) Conference: *Creative Hearts, Healing Minds*. His poems have appeared recently in *Fresh, Aries, Nantahala, The New St. Andrews Review, Pembroke, The Asheville Poetry Review* and others. Roberts received a B.A. from UNC-Chapel Hill and a M.A. from Hollins College, where he received the Hollins College Graduate Fellowship and the Claytor Award for Poetry. His work has been nominated for a Pushcart Prize and received an Academy of American Poets Prize. He has been awarded the George Mason University Graduate Fellowship, as well as fellowships at the Hambidge Center, the Weymouth Center, and the Virginia Center for the Creative Arts, and in 1999 was selected by the North Carolina Writer's Network as a Blumenthal Reader. Roberts has served as an adjunct professor of English at the University of Richmond, the University of North Carolina at Wilmington, and Cape Fear Community College. He grew up in Winston-Salem, N. C., and lives in Wilmington, where he is a member of the Screen Actors Guild and the International Association of Theatrical Stage Employees.

JENNIFER ROSE was born in Evanston, Illinois. She received her B.A. in English and Communications from Simmons College, an M.A. in Creative Writing and an M.U.A. in urban planning from Boston University. Her poems have appeared in *Poetry, The Nation, Ploughshares* and elsewhere. She has received grants and fellowships from the NEA, Massachusetts Cultural Council and Astraea Foundation, among others. Rose is the author of two books of poetry, *The Old Direction of Heaven* (Truman State University Press, 2000) and *Hometown for an Hour* (Ohio University Press, 2006), winner of the Hollis Summers Award and the Audre Lorde Poetry Prize. She works as a city planner specializing in downtown revitalization. Rose was a Fellow at VCCA in 1993, a time she remembers fondly not only for its beauty and productivity but also for the ongoing friendship made there between her and the artist with whom she shared an adjoining bathroom.

THADDEUS RUTKOWSKI was born in Kingston, Pennsylvania, and is a graduate of Cornell University and The Johns Hopkins University. He is the author of three novels, *Haywire* (Starcherone), *Tetched* (Behler) and *Roughhouse* (Kaya*)*. His first two books were finalists for a Members' Choice Asian American Literary Award. He teaches literature at the City University of New York and fiction writing at the Writer's Voice of the West Side YMCA in Manhattan. He has been the fiction editor for the literary magazine *Many Mountains Moving* since 2007.

NEIL SHEPARD was born in Fitchburg, Massachusetts. He has published three books of poetry: *Scavenging the Country for a Heartbeat* (First Book Award, Mid-List Press, 1993); *I'm Here Because I Lost My Way* (Mid-List, 1998); and *This Far from the Source* (Mid-List, 2006). His fourth book, *Travel/Untravel*, is due in 2011 from Mid-List. His poems appear in literary magazines such as *Boulevard, Harvard Review, New England Review, North American Review, Ploughshares, Paris Review, Shenandoah, Southern Review*, and *TriQuarterly*, as well as online at *Poetry Daily* and *Verse Daily*. He founded the Writers Program at the Vermont Studio Center and directed it for eight years. He now teaches in the low-residency M.F.A. Writing Program at Wilkes University (Pennsylvania), and he is the long-time editor of *Green Mountains Review*.

ENID SHOMER was born in Washington, D.C. She is the author of seven books. Her stories and poems have appeared in *The New Yorker, The Atlantic, Poetry, Best American Poetry, Paris Review, New Stories from the South: the Year's Best, etc.* and more than seventy anthologies and textbooks. Her poetry books are: *Stalking the Florida Panther* (Winner of the Word Works Prize); *This Close to the Earth*; *Black Drum;* and *Stars at Noon: Poems from the Life of Jacqueline Cochran* (all from University of Arkansas Press). *Imaginary Men* won the Iowa Prize and the LSU/*Southern Review* Prize, both given for a first work of fiction by an American. *Tourist Season* (Random House, 2007) won the Gold Medal in Fiction from the state of Florida and was chosen for Barnes & Noble's "Discover Great Writers" program. Her feature interviews on National Public Radio are available online: the first (from "All Things Considered") for *Imaginary Men,* the second (from Sunday's "Morning Edition") for her poem-biography *Stars at Noon: Poems from the Life of Jacqueline Cochran.* The recipient of two grants in poetry from the NEA and three grants from the state of Florida, Shomer edits the University of Arkansas Poetry Series and has taught as a visiting writer at the Ohio State University, Florida State, University of Arkansas, and others. Her debut novel, *The Twelve Rooms of the Nile* is forthcoming in 2012 from Simon and Schuster.

TAIJE SILVERMAN was born in San Francisco, California. She is currently the 2010-2011 W. K. Rose Fellow through Vassar College, and a 2011 Fulbright Fellow at the University of Bologna. Her first book, *Houses Are Fields*, was published in 2009.

MELISSA STEIN was born near Philadelphia. She is the author of the poetry collection *Rough Honey*, winner of the 2010 APR/Honickman First Book Prize. Her poems have appeared in *The Southern Review, New England Review, Best New Poets 2009, Harvard Review, North American Review*, and many other journals and anthologies. She has received residency fellowships from Yaddo, the MacDowell Colony, and the Djerassi Foundation, and her work has won awards from *Spoon River Poetry Review, Literal Latté*, and the Dorothy Sargent Rosenberg Foundation, among others. She holds an M.A. in creative writing from the University of California at Davis, and is a freelance editor and writer in San Francisco.

ELISABETH STEVENS was born in Rome, New York. She is a writer of fiction and poetry, as well as drama, art, film, and book reviews. A contributing arts writer for Sarasota's Arts and Culture magazine, she also creates and exhibits etchings, linocuts, ink drawings, silverpoints, and other graphics. She is the author of ten collections of poetry and short stories.

STEPHEN TAPSCOTT was born in Iowa. He's the author of five books of poems and several books of translations (including the *Love Sonnets* of Pablo Neruda and the war-elegies of Georg Trakl). He just returned to America after a stint as a visiting professor at Balliol College, Oxford.

Of this poem, Tapscott writes: "'Mud' was written, clearly I guess, in that midwinter-spring that happens in the Blue Ridge/VCCA hills in January-February —it's mist-season, in which details of the landscape seem temporarily blurry, but one's sense of self somehow sharpens in response to the softening of lines in the external world—a kind of paysage moralisé that I know nowhere else. The cows were still an active presence in the pasture, too, a presence which intensified that sense that the landscape was almost talking to you...maybe because a cow would come looming up to you out of the cold fog, even on the drive up the hill. The long lines and denotative factuality of the tone were experiments I was working on, imitating poems of Czeslaw Milosz, who actually came to lunch at VCCA that January!"

ALICE TEMPLETON was born in Memphis, Tennessee. Since 2002 she has lived in San Francisco, California, where she teaches creative writing and literature at the Art Institute of California-San Francisco. Her poems have appeared in *Poetry*, *88*, *Puerto del Sol*, *Many Mountains Moving*, and elsewhere. Her chapbook *Archaeology* won the 2008 New Women's Voices Prize in Poetry from Finishing Line Press.

"'Song Beside the Barn Wall' was written in 1997, during my first residency at VCCA," Templeton writes. "I would eat lunch on the steps of my studio (the corn crib) and admire the milk barn, which, with its concrete and stone walls, was quite different from the wooden, dirt-floor barns familiar to me in Tennessee. At that time I was a working songwriter and musician, and was trying to create poetry carried as much by its music as by its meaning. The poem was originally part of a series of lyrics/songs written in and for specific ordinary locations. I found its form in the six-accent line."

VIVIAN TETER was born in Midwest City, Oklahoma. Her chapbook, *Translating a Bridge*, was written at Virginia Center for the Creative Arts and published in 2007 by Toadlily Press of Chappaqua, New York immediately after her VCCA fellowship. Her poetry has appeared in *Spoon River*, *The Missouri Review*, *Poetry East*, *The Gettysburg Review*, *The Anglican Theological Review*, *Other Voices International Poetry Project*, *Green Mountains Review*, *Passages North* and other journals. Currently a professor in the English Department at Virginia Wesleyan College in Norfolk, Virginia, she holds an M.F.A. from the University of Arizona and a B.A. from Hollins University. She has received two Pushcart Prize nominations.

J. C. TODD was born in Brooklyn, New York. She is the author of three volumes of poetry, *What Space This Body* (2008), *Nightshade*, and *Entering Pisces*. She teaches creative writing at Bryn Mawr College and in the M.F.A. in Creative Writing program at Rosemont College, both in eastern Pennsylvania. Awards include an Individual Artist Fellowship in Poetry from the Pennsylvania Council on the Arts, and two awards from the Leeway Foundation as well as an International Artist Fellowship to Schloss Wiepersdorf in Germany from VCCA.

ALISON TOWNSEND was born in Allentown, Pennsylvania. She is the author of two books of poetry, *Persephone in America*, which won the Crab Orchard Open Poetry Competition (Southern Illinois University Press, 2009), and *The Blue Dress*, selected for the Marie Alexander Prose Poem series (White Pine Press, 2003; second edition, 2008). She also has two limited edition chapbooks, *And Still the Music* (Flume Press winner, 2006-2007), and *What the Body Knows* (Parallel Press, 2002). Her poetry and creative nonfiction appear widely, in journals such as *Crab Orchard Review, Margie, Rattle, Arts & Letters, Fourth Genre*, and *Southern Review*, and anthologies such as *Wildbranch: An Anthology of Nature, Environmental, and Place-Based Writing, Claiming the Spirit Within*, and *The House of Your Dream, Boomer Girls*, and *Flash Fiction Forward*. She has won many awards, including a Pushcart Prize, publication in *Best American Poetry*, and literary fellowships from the Wisconsin Arts Board, Norcroft, Hedgebrook, and the Virginia Center for the Creative Arts. She teaches English, creative writing and women's studies at the University of Wisconsin-Whitewater. She lives with her husband on four acres of prairie and oak savanna in the farm country outside Madison, and is currently working on *Mapping Home Ground*, a collection of lyric essays about place.

MARTIN TUCKER was born in Philadelphia, Pennsylvania. He has published four collections of poetry, the most recent *Plenty Of Exits* (2009). He is the author of five works of literary criticism, among them the widely-praised *Literary Exile In The Twentieth Century*. He has edited more than 20 volumes of literary encyclopedias. His plays have been produced in the U.S. and England. He retired from the editorship of *Confrontation* Magazine this year after 42 years at the helm. He is Professor Emeritus of Long Island University.

MEMYE CURTIS TUCKER was born in Atlanta, Georgia. A VCCA Resident Fellow in 1993 and 2002, she is the author of *The Watchers* (Hollis Summers Poetry Prize, Ohio University Press, 1998) and the prizewinning chapbooks *Admit One* (State Street Press), *Storm Line* (Palanquin Press), and *Holding Patterns* (Poetry Atlanta Press). Her poems have appeared in numerous print journals and anthologies, and have been set as art song and featured in translation abroad. In 2007, she received the Lifetime Achievement Award from the Georgia Writers Association. In 2010 the Georgia Center for the Book named *The Watchers* one of

"The Twenty-five Books All Georgians Should Read." Also a MacDowell Fellow, she holds a Ph.D. in English Literature, teaches advanced poetry writing at Atlanta's Callanwolde Fine Arts Center, and is a Senior Editor of *Atlanta Review.*

"One summer morning at VCCA," Tucker writes, "I noticed an unusual arrangement atop one of the stelae that make VCCA's grounds a kind of sculpture garden. Combed grasses and oval stones had been placed there deliberately, as if in offering. But whose petition? To whom? Why? Humans have always bargained, promised, offered sacrifices: any of us could have been asking for help in our work. I remembered how much the dying, even more, long for a miracle. That night, it rained, and outside the door of my studio, the afternoon's feathery orbs of seeded dandelions were torn apart. An answer, if not a final one."

G. C. WALDREP was born in South Boston, Virginia. His collections of poetry include *Goldbeater's Skin* (2003, winner of the Colorado Prize); *Disclamor* (BOA Editions, 2007); *Archicembalo* (Tupelo Press, 2009, winner of the Dorset Prize); and, with John Gallaher, *Your Father on the Train of Ghosts* (BOA Editions, 2011). He lives in Lewisburg, Pennsylvania, and teaches at Bucknell University.

"Tropic of Cancer" was written when Waldrep was in residence at VCCA in October and November, 2001. The poem took as its point of departure a bit of sheet music Waldrep found taped to the wall of his studio, the Corncrib.

BJ WARD was born in Union, New Jersey. He is the author of three books of poetry: *Gravedigger's Birthday*, *17 Love Poems with No Despair*, and *Landing in New Jersey with Soft Hands*, all published by North Atlantic Books. His poetry has been featured on *Poetry Daily* and National Public Radio's "The Writer's Almanac," as well as in publications such as *Poetry, 5 AM, TriQuarterly, Green Mountains Review, The Literary Review, Mid-American Review, Puerto Del Sol, Painted Bride Quarterly, The Sun*, and a host of other journals. His essays have appeared in *The New York Times, The Worcester Review, Teaching Artist Journal, Inside Jersey,* and the American Library Association's main advocacy web site, *ilovelibraries.org.* He is the recipient of a Pushcart Prize and two Distinguished Artist Fellowships from the NJ State Council on the Arts. He lives with his wife and son in Changewater, New Jersey, and teaches in the Creative Writing program at Warren County Community College.

MARJORY WENTWORTH was born in Lynn, Massachusetts. In 2003, she was named South Carolina's Poet Laureate for life. She is the author of two collections of poetry and one poetry chapbook.

MICHELE WOLF was born in Denville, New Jersey. She is the author of *Immersion,* chosen by Denise Duhamel for the Hilary Tham Capital Collection and published by The Word Works. Her previous books are *Conversations During Sleep,* winner of the Anhinga Prize for Poetry and published by Anhinga Press, and *The Keeper of Light,* selected for the *Painted Bride Quarterly* Poetry Chapbook Series. Her poems have appeared in *Poetry, The Hudson Review, Boulevard,* and many other literary journals and anthologies, including the award-winning *When I Am an Old Woman I Shall Wear Purple.* She serves as a contributing editor for *Poet Lore.* Among her honors are two residencies at VCCA. An editor and a longtime workshop leader at The Writer's Center in Bethesda, she lives with her husband and daughter in Gaithersburg, Maryland.

ACKNOWLEDGMENTS

The editors wish to thank Fellows Council Chair Karen Bell, Lexie Boris, Ted Craddock, Kelly Cherry, Tom Drescher, Dana Jones, Suny Monk, Craig Pleasants, Julia Pleasants, Sheila Gulley Pleasants, and Dan Vera, as well as the entire staff at VCCA for their enthusiasm and assistance. On behalf of VCCA, we thank the National Endowment for the Arts and the Virginia Commission for the Arts for their ongoing support.

We are especially grateful to Bernard Handzel and Karen Bell, whose beautiful photographs of VCCA grace our front and back covers.

Grateful acknowledgment is made to the magazines and collections in which these poems previously appeared and to the editors who selected them. A sincere attempt has been made to locate all copyright holders. Unless otherwise noted, copyright to the poems is held by the individual poets.

Marcia Aldrich: "Spring Comes to Virginia" appeared in *Northwest Review*. Reprinted by permission of the poet.

Karren LaLonde Alenier: "Retreat" from *Looking for Divine Transportation*, The Bunny & Crocodile Press. ©1999 by Karren LaLonde Alenier. Reprinted by permission of the poet.

Annette Allen: "After the Ice Storm" from *Country of Light*, Mount Olive College Press. © 1998 by Annette Allen. Reprinted by permission of the poet.

Rebecca Baggett: "God and the Artists' Colony" from *Claiming the Spirit Within*, Beacon Press. ©1996 by Rebecca Baggett. Also appeared in *God Puts on the Body of a Deer*, Main Street Rag. ©2010 by Rebecca Baggett. Reprinted by permission of the poet.

Ned Balbo: "The Minor Hours," Sibelius Music. Reprinted by permission of the poet.

Mary Bonina: "Lines Inspired by a Horse" from *Clear Eye Tea*, Cervena Barva Press. © 2010 by Mary Bonina. Reprinted by permission of the poet.

Andrea Carter Brown: "Blues, For Bill" from *Blues For Bill: A Tribute to William Matthews*, University of Akron Press. Also appeared in *Ploughshares*. Reprinted by permission of the poet.

Andrea Hollander Budy: "Writing Studio" appeared in *The Georgia Review*. Reprinted by permission of the poet.

Fran Castan: "Giant Beech at Sweet Briar, February" appeared in *The Napa Review*. Reprinted by permission of the poet.

Kelly Cherry: "The Bright Field" appeared in *Cave Wall*. Reprinted by permission of the poet.

Patricia Clark: "Across Barbed Wire" from *Imagination & Place Anthology*, Imagination & Place Press. Reprinted by permission of the poet.

Barbara Crooker: "The VCCA Fellows Visit the Holiness Baptist Church, Amherst, Virginia" from *Line Dance*, Word Press. © 2008 by Barbara Crooker. Also appeared in *Christianity and Literature*. Reprinted by permission of the poet.

Deborah Cummins: "Before It's Too Late" from *Counting the Wave*, Word Tech Press. © 2008 by Deborah Cummins. Reprinted by permission of the poet.

Carol V. Davis: "Driving Through Rural Virginia" from *It's Time to Talk About…*, Symposium. ©1996 by Carol V. Davis. Also appeared in *Hawaii Pacific Review*. Reprinted by permission of the poet.

Carla Drysdale: "New Year's Eve at the Artists' Colony" from *Little Venus*, Tightrope Books. Reprinted by permission of the poet.

Moira Egan: "Hearts & Stones" from *Discovering Genre: Poetry*, Prestwick House. Also appeared in *Spin*, Entasis Press, and *Rip the Page! Adventures in Creative Writing*, Shambhala Publications. Reprinted by permission of the poet.

George Ellenbogen: "Buzzards by a Dead Dog" from *The Rhino Gate and Other Poems*, Vehicule Press. Also appeared in *Morning Gothic: New and Selected Poems*, Vehicule Press. Reprinted by permission of the poet.

Charles Fishman: "A Field in Virginia" from *A Field in Virginia*, Uccelli Press, 2004. Also appeared in *Pedestal Magazine*. Reprinted by permission of the poet.

Alice Friman: "Eyesore" appeared in *Margie*. Reprinted by permission of the poet.

Becky Gould Gibson: "Summer Solstice in Pastels" appeared in *Chiron Review*. Reprinted by permission of the poet.

L. B. Green: "Of Work and Song on Mt. San Angelo" appeared in *Night Garden*. Reprinted by permission of the poet.

Ralph Grüneberger: "Old Virginia" from *The Mystery is: You are and you are not. American Poems*, Aphaia Verlag, Berlin. Reprinted by permission of the poet.

Kenneth Hart: "Women's College" appeared in *New Ohio Review*. Reprinted by permission of the poet.

Neva Herrington: "Woodchuck at the Art Colony" from *Her BMW and Other Poems*, Pudding House Publications. Also appeared in *The Chariton Review*. Reprinted by permission of the poet.

Con Hilberry: "Virginia Night" appeared in *Dunes Review*. Reprinted by permission of the poet.

Lori Horvitz: "Art Colony Birthday Party" appeared in *Facets Magazine*. Reprinted by permission of the poet.

Colette Inez: "Witness to a Meadow in Virginia" appeared in *Neo*. Reprinted by permission of the poet.

Margaret B. Ingraham: "Proverbs" appeared in *Nimrod International Journal*. Reprinted by permission of the poet.

Halvard Johnson: "Old Virginia Trees" from *Organ Harvest with Entrance of Clones*, Hamilton Stone Editions. Reprinted by permission of the poet.

Marilyn Kallet: "Ode to the Open Window (Sweet Briar)" from *Packing Light: New and Selected Poems*, Black Widow Press. Reprinted by permission of the poet.

LuAnn Keener-Mikenas: "Sweet Briar Colony, the Lovers" appeared in *Quarterly West*. Reprinted by permission of the poet.

Sybil Kollar: "The Cows (Sweet Briar)" appeared in *New Millennium Writings*. Reprinted by permission of the poet.

Angela Kreuz: "eternal moment" from *uns auf schwingen*, Gedok. Reprinted by permission of the poet.

Laurie Kutchins: "Summerless" from *The Night Path*, BOA Editions. Also appeared in *Poetry*. Reprinted by permission of the poet.

Teresa Leo: "Virginia Farm Haunting" appeared in *The Country Dog Review*. Reprinted by permission of the poet.

Ginny MacKenzie: "No Leash Law" appeared in *Prairie Schooner*. Reprinted by permission of the poet.

Mary Mackey: "Lynchburg" from *Breaking the Fever*, Marsh Hawk Press. Reprinted by permission of the poet.

Elizabeth Seydel Morgan: "The Place You Left" from *Governor of Desire*, Louisiana State University Press. ©1993 by Elizabeth Seydel Morgan. Reprinted by permission of Louisiana State University Press.

Tanure Ojaide: "At Mt. San Angelo, outside the real world" from *The Beauty I Have Seen: A Trilogy*, Malthouse Press. Reprinted by permission of the poet.

Kathleen O'Toole: "Winter of Ice and Straw" from *Meanwhile*, David Roberts Books. Reprinted by permission of the poet.

Lia Purpura: "Era" appeared in *Indiana Review*. Reprinted by permission of the poet.

Kim Roberts: "Darwin in Reverse" from *The Wishbone Galaxy*, Washington Writer's Publishing House. Also appeared in *Hometown for an Hour*, Ohio University Press. Reprinted by permission of the poet.

Steve Roberts: "Knowledge of Cows" from *A Space Inside A Space*, St. Andrews Press. Reprinted by permission of the poet.

Jennifer Rose: "Mt. San Angelo Postcard" from *Hometown for an Hour*, Ohio University Press. Reprinted by permission of the poet.

Thaddeus Rutkowski: "Leaping Buck Icons" appeared in *Mobius: The Poetry Magazine*. Reprinted by permission of the poet.

Neil Shepard: "This Is How It Is" from *This Far from the Source*, Mid-List Press. Also appeared in *Poetry Daily*. Reprinted by permission of the poet.

Enid Shomer: "Among the Cows" from *This Close to the Earth*, Arkansas University Press. © 1992 by Enid Shomer. Reprinted by permission of Arkansas University Press.

Taije Silverman: "On Joy" from *Houses Are Fields*, Louisiana State University Press. © 2009 by Taije Silverman. Reprinted by permission of Louisiana State University Press. Also appeared in *Ploughshares*.

Melissa Stein: "Anaphylaxis" from *Rough Honey*, *American Poetry Review*. Reprinted by permission of the poet.

Elisabeth Stevens: "Swimming to the Dam" from *Night Lover, Art & Poetry*, Birch Brook Press. Reprinted by permission of the poet.

Stephen Tapscott: "Mud" from *From the Book of Changes*, Carnegie-Mellon University Press. Reprinted by permission of the poet.

Alice Templeton: "Song Beside the Barn Wall" appeared in *Poetry*. Reprinted by permission of the poet.

Vivian Teter: "Notes on Hunger at the Artists' Colony" appeared in *Virginia Wesleyan Review*. Reprinted by permission of the poet.

J. C. Todd: "Spring Ephemerals" from *What Space This Body*, Wind Publications. Reprinted by permission of the poet.

Alison Townsend: "Reading the Famous Woman Poet's New Book, also about Persephone, on First Day of Spring" from *Persephone in America*, Southern Illinois University Press. Reprinted by permission of the poet.

Martin Tucker: "On Leaving an Artists' Colony" from *Attention Spans*, Confrontation Press. Reprinted by permission of the poet.

Memye Curtis Tucker: "Rubato" from *The Watchers*, Ohio University Press. Reprinted by permission of the poet.

G. C. Waldrep: "Tropic of Cancer" from *Goldbeater's Skin*, Center for Literary Publishing. Reprinted by permission of the poet.

BJ Ward: "Upon Being Told Again There Are No Rhymes For Certain Words" from *Gravedigger's Birthday*, North Atlantic Books. Reprinted by permission of the poet.

Marjory Heath Wentworth: "Stillborn" from *The Endless Repetition of an Ordinary Miracle*, Press 53. Also appeared in *The Southern Women's Review*. Reprinted by permission of the poet.

Michele Wolf: "Night Vision" from *Conversations During Sleep*, Anhinga Press. Also appeared in *Hubbub* and *Keeper of Light*, from *Painted Bride Quarterly*. Reprinted by permission of the poet.

ABOUT VCCA

Nestled in the rolling foothills of Virginia's Blue Ridge Mountains, VCCA is one of the largest artists' communities in the nation. Each year, it provides more than 350 residential fellowships to writers, composers and visual artists from across the country and around the world. For forty years, the books, music and art created by VCCA Fellows have filled libraries, concert halls and galleries around the globe, and have garnered just about every prestigious award including the Pulitzer Prize and MacArthur "Genius Award."

Writers Elizabeth Coles Langhorne and Nancy Hale founded VCCA (Virginia Center for the Creative Arts) in 1971 at Wavertree Farm in Charlottesville, Virginia. In the fall of 1977, Sweet Briar College, a vibrant liberal arts women's college founded in 1901 in Amherst, Virginia, agreed to lease the adjacent grounds of Mt. San Angelo to VCCA. This began a long term collaboration on several mutually beneficial programs that continue to bring writers, visual artists and composers to VCCA and Sweet Briar.

Today, VCCA operates America's largest international artists' residency exchange program and is one of only three artists' residencies in the world with facilities in two continents: Mt. San Angelo in Amherst, Virginia and Moulin à Nef in Auvillar, France.

Visit us at vcca.com.

www.ingramcontent.com/pod-product-compliance
Lightning Source LLC
Chambersburg PA
CBHW032102080426
42733CB00006B/386